Some
Good !

Some Good!

Treasured secrets from Nova Scotia's favourite country restaurants

Judith Comfort

NIMBUS PUBLISHING LIMITED

Editorial and Concept: Judith Comfort and Graphic Design Associates
Cover Photo: George Georgakakos
Text illustrations: Kevin Sollows
Design and production: Graphic Design Associates
Printed in Nova Scotia, Canada
Published and distributed by Nimbus Publishing Limited,
Post Office Box 9301, Station A, Halifax, Nova Scotia B3K 5N5

4th Printing, 1991

Canadian Cataloguing in Publication Data

Comfort, Judith
    Some good!

ISBN 0-920852-37-8.
1. Restaurants, lunch rooms, etc. — Nova Scotia
2. Cookery, Canadian — Nova Scotia. I. Title.

TX910.C2C65 1985   647'.95716   C85-098449-1

Some good / adv, N.S., dialect   **1:** to a high degree
(EXTREMELY good) (VERY good)   **2:** in actual fact
(TRULY good) / comp form: right some good   / superl form:
right some jaysus good / usually expressed with gusto,
relish, zest, and a hint of irony /

For generations of cooks:
Basheva, Ruth, Anna Basheva, Lillian Ruth, and Esme Ruth

Contents

Appetizers

Soups

Meat and Poultry / Main Course

Fish and Shellfish / Main Course

Lighter Dishes

Breads

Cakes and Pies

Desserts

Beverages

Acknowledgements:

Alan Comfort who shared every mile, morsel, and word of this book along the way, and never once complained.
Steven Slipp whose professionalism and sensitivity brought the project together.
Wendy Elliott who edited the manuscript, and more.
Cynthia Wine and Alice Trillin who pushed me in the right direction.
Kathy Chute who proofread recipes all times of day and night.
Kathleen Evans who typed the manuscript.
Thank you

Some good places to eat in Nova Scotia

Amherst Shore Country Inn
Lorneville, 32 km east of Amherst
on Highway 366
(902) 667-4800

Balmoral Motel
Tatamagouche, Highway 6
(902) 657-2000

Blomidon Inn
Wolfville, 127 Main St.
(902) 542-9326

The Bright House
Sherbrooke, Highway 7
(902) 522-2691

The Cape House Inn
Mahone Bay, Highway 3
(902) 624-8211

Evangeline Snack Bar
Grand Pré, 4 km east of Wolfville,
on Highway 1
(902) 542-2703

Garrison House Inn
Annapolis Royal, 350 George St.
(902) 532-5750

Gladee's Canteen and Restaurant
Hirtle's Beach, near Kingsburg, off
Highway 332,
10 km south of Lunenburg
(902) 766-4430

Gramma's House
Port Saxon, off Highway 3, midway
between Barrington and Shelburne
(902) 637-2058

Harris' Seafood Restaurant
Dayton, 3 km north of Yarmouth
on Highway 1
(902) 742-5420

MacLeod's Canteen
Green Bay, off Highway 331, 2 km
southeast of Petite Riviere
(902) 688-2212

Marquis of Dufferin Lodge and Motel
Port Dufferin, on Highway 7, 14 km
east of Sheet Harbour
(902) 654-2696

Mets Acadiens
Cheticamp, Highway 19
(902) 224-2170

Milford House
South Milford, 20 km south of
Annapolis Royal on Highway 8
(902) 532-2617

The Normaway Inn
N.E. Margaree, on Egypt Road,
midway between Lake O'Law and
Margaree Valley
(902) 248-2987

The Palliser
Truro, 4 km west of town centre on
Highway 102 at exit 14
(902) 893-8951

Roadside Grill
Belliveau Cove, on Highway 1,
5 km west of Weymouth
(902) 837-5047

Telegraph House
Baddeck, Chebucto St.
(902) 295-9988

The Whitman Inn
Kempt, on Highway 8, 4 km south of
Kejimkujik National Park
(902) 242-2226

Zwicker's Inn
Mahone Bay, 662 Main St.
(902) 624-8045

Some good places to eat in Nova Scotia

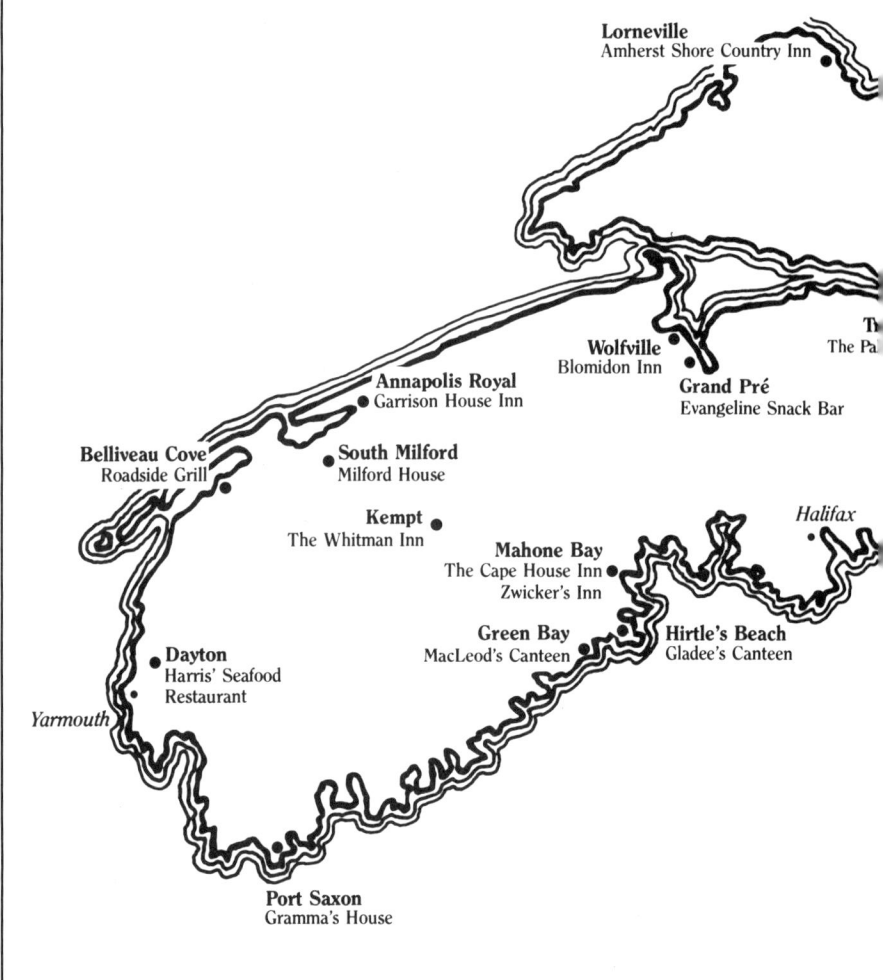

Lorneville
Amherst Shore Country Inn

Wolfville
Blomidon Inn

Tr
The Pa

Annapolis Royal
Garrison House Inn

Grand Pré
Evangeline Snack Bar

Belliveau Cove
Roadside Grill

South Milford
Milford House

Halifax

Kempt
The Whitman Inn

Mahone Bay
The Cape House Inn
Zwicker's Inn

Dayton
Harris' Seafood
Restaurant

Green Bay
MacLeod's Canteen

Hirtle's Beach
Gladee's Canteen

Yarmouth

Port Saxon
Gramma's House

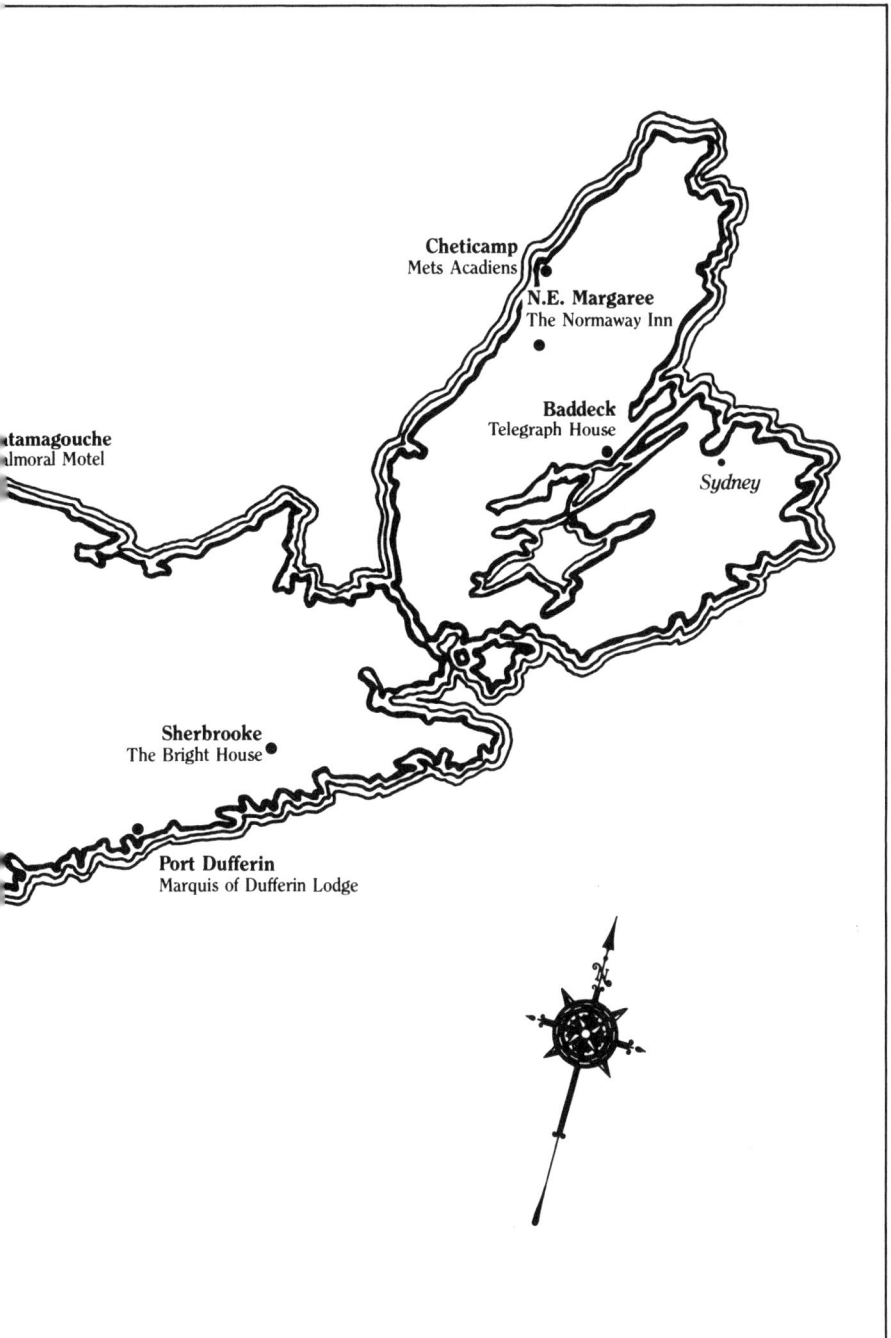

Cheticamp
Mets Acadiens

N.E. Margaree
The Normaway Inn

Baddeck
Telegraph House

Sydney

tamagouche
lmoral Motel

Sherbrooke
The Bright House

Port Dufferin
Marquis of Dufferin Lodge

N

Foreword

To eat well in Nova Scotia, you have to know someone. It's one thing to find the spiffy places that serve corporate clams and play hide-the-haddock, but getting to those rare dining rooms that have the real stuff — the food that Nova Scotians claim to ache for after they've moved west for better jobs and worse meals — is harder. Someone has to show you where they are.

Judith Comfort is just the person to do it. I've eaten a lot of meals in Judith's kitchen in Port Medway and she would never serve a halibut that wasn't perfect, a blueberry grunt that wasn't great. She wouldn't eat it in a restaurant either.

This book is about people who cook restaurant food home-style. Like Miss Marjorie Stirling who has baked cherry pie the same way for 35 years, so there's no improving on it. And James Hawerychuk who, while he was growing up on the Prairies, might never have guessed he'd one day earn his living transforming buckets of Atlantic potatoes into Acadian rappie pie. And 80-year-old Leita Aulenback who picks the famous Nova Scotia wild blueberries for Bright House pies.

Each of the twenty restaurants in this book has behind it the story of people who have abandoned sleep — and sometimes solvency — to open their successful dream restaurant: Gwynneth Turnbull has such a fine rapport with her staff, they call her "mother"; Jean Turner raised her children first, then bought back the house in which she was born and turned it into a bed and breakfast. She cooks full course dinners every night — without a cookbook.

The restaurants are successful because of their loyal diners. The 'regulars' at the Palliser in Truro includes a couple in their nineites who drive up from Dartmouth every Sunday to sit at their favourite table and to eat their favourite dishes served by their favourite waitress. The Breck family are regulars who have returned to the Milford House for five generations.

From her years as a fussy cook, Judith knows how to avoid the fried fish and find where they poach it fresh and serve it with a little lemon juice. She also happens to know who serves the best clam chowder in the province, if not the country. She's tasted it, talked to the folks who made it, coaxed the recipes from them and brought it home to test in her kitchen that has a real brick oven that Alan Comfort built brick by brick.

This is a wonderful book — a Maritime *Michelin* filled with all sorts of information about good restaurants and how to cook what they make best. I wish I'd thought of it myself, but Judith Comfort ate there first.

Cynthia Wine

Introduction

Like Anna Redgrave, owner of the Garrison House Inn, I also had a grandmother who ran a summer boarding house. As a young widow she worked sixteen hour days and made a modest living. But by the time I was born, the dozens of cinnamon buns that would come out of her oven were reserved for children and grandchildren, who might just happen by. Lucky us, for there was a bond between food, family and pleasure.

My mother was also a great cook, but because she grew up washing dishes at the boarding house (when they hauled water in buckets and heated it up on a wood stove), she was never tempted to share her cooking with anyone but her family and friends.

But the negative side of things tends to mellow out in a couple of generations, and I have always been a hopeless romantic about restaurants. I started this project because I thought it would be great fun to check out twenty different places in one summer. Where other people might like to get behind the scenes of a movie set, or a brewery, I was excited at the idea of seeing the nether world of the public restaurant — the kitchen. I would talk to the owners and extract their trade secrets. And I wanted their recipes — especially Jack Sorensen's recipe for mussel soup!

The owners were kind. They showed me their kitchens, their homes, and more. I recall sitting in an overstuffed chair in the Hirtle parlor, cozy with generations of family possessions. Spry, eighty-year-old Flossie perched on the edge of my chair. Her arm was around me as she pointed to the photos in the family album I held in my lap.

Gale Hastings gave me two hours of her time and philosophy in the comfort of her beautifully furnished living room. It was the middle of a hectic tourist season and on that day she and her husband Peter were trying to escape for a few hours to celebrate their wedding anniversary.

When I called to make an appointment to see Warren Miller at the end of the season, he commented that there'd be no telling where he'd be the day after closing up Milford House. He'd be gone fishing.

What I found was twenty small family businesses. Each one was unique. Their names reflected differences in style and vintage — restaurant, snack bar, grill, canteen, inn. Many of the owners worked sixteen hour days, and made modest livings. Over half of them were hopeless romantics who had come from other professions: teachers, nurses, musicians, engineers.

I looked for places that were not disposed towards prefrozen refried fish, edible oil products, canned gravies and peas; who avoided medleys of substandard ingredients blended together to make the lowest common denominator.

By word-of-mouth I searched out public eating establishments that served fish that still had a wiggle in it. I longed for bread, soft and warm out of the oven (not vulcanized out of the microwave). And blueberry pie with the perfume of berries fresh off the barrens (not canned blue glue).

Restaurant cooking is by definition institutional cooking. It requires different tools and methods to produce larger quantities than home cooking. It is easy to see why much institutional cooking has succumbed to the use of high food technology to produce inferior results, but with increased efficiency and profits.

But a small family-centred business is different. Owners know and care about diners. Local suppliers can provide quality ingredients. Quantities prepared are small. Owners are involved in every aspect of the business from bookkeeping to dishwashing. But most important of all, profit is not always the primary goal. It is possible to serve a meal that is close to real home cooked food.

I have deep respect for these people, who have put their time, energies and souls into doing what many of us have always wanted to do — open up a restaurant.

Amherst Shore Country Inn
Lorneville

During the winter Jim and Donna Laceby of the Amherst Shore Country Inn often give dinner parties for their friends. Donna, a gifted cook, prepares a never-tried-before soup, bread, entree and dessert. Her guests then get the rare opportunity to tell their hostess what they really think of her cooking. The recipes fall into two categories: *the keepers* (like her fresh sliced mushroom soup) and those that *need more work*. From this 'research' evolves next year's menu for the Amherst Shore Country Inn.

Every night is dinner party night during the busy summer months. The twenty-five or so guests may pay for their meal, but Donna prepares an elegant dinner much the same way she would for her own friends. There is only one sitting, at 7:30 p.m., which means diners have the table for the evening. There is no rush. They can relax and enjoy the gorgeous view of the Northumberland Strait and Jim's golden-oldies piano along with their dessert.

In fact, the Lacebys have a good many loyal year-round customers from as far away as Truro, Moncton and Sackville, who entertain their friends at the Amherst Shore Country Inn rather than at home. While making reservations they plan the dinner menu with Donna. Their choice includes eighteen entrees such as ragout of beef with celery and walnuts, chicken Veronique (grapes, honey and orange) and seven soups, salads and intricate desserts. The recipe for one favorite, amaretto chocolate cheesecake, was published in the September 1984 issue of *Gourmet*.

Donna describes her cooking style as European, primarily French and Italian. The recipes she uses are complex but results are light, not overstated or overcooked. She has a natural sense of balance in her cooking. Jim says that *'she uses cream and butter to enhance the food, not to impress the guests.'*

The single dinner sitting — everyone served the same meal at once — makes for a simple, fast delivery system from the kitchen point of view. Jim says this system allows them to control the food quality and avoid waste. Simplicity is essential. Outside of a little help with cleanup and service, Donna manages the kitchen on her own. She starts after breakfast baking the Viennese breaded loaves, oatmeal bread (with an interesting touch of cinnamon), and the rich, luxurious desserts. She may have a break around lunchtime, to have a cup of tea with a friend or lie in the sun, but because she does all the cooking, never has a day off. At dinner time Jim pours the wine while Donna puts final touches on the platters of food. A waitress may serve the entree, but it is likely that Donna will pour the last cup of coffee.

Although there is a tremendous amount of hard work, Donna and Jim say there are advantages to having things totally under their control. Less hassle and expense is involved in doing it themselves rather than hiring other people. Jim says that being small has forced them to be efficient.

If this sounds like good sound business sense, it is — Jim's background is in business. The Lacebys originally moved from Ontario when Jim opened up the new Lifesavers chewing gum plant in Amherst. They bought the former Weeks Lodge as a family home for themselves and their five children, but Donna became intrigued with the idea of running it as a tourist home again.

The Lacebys' background also includes a 400 acre Ontario farm. They have been able to apply their farming knowledge to the business today. Their diningroom is one of the very few in Nova Scotia that serves fresh vegetables within view of the garden where they are grown. The garden is huge and through successive plantings and the children's help, they are able to serve fresh brussels sprouts, celery, romaine and spinach almost until Christmas. They also have a small greenhouse for starting plants and a storage shed for carrots, squash and root crops. Jim says, *'If a vegetable is out of season, we don't serve it.'*

A few years ago the Lacebys took a tour of twenty country inns in New England, talking to the owners and guests, making plans for their own inn. It is obvious that with Jim's business management, Donna's wonderful ability in the kitchen and the children's help, they have hit on a successful combination at the Amherst Shore Country Inn.

Chicken Breast with Spicy Wild Rice Dressing

4 large **chicken breasts** with bone in and a good covering of skin
10 Tbsp (175 mL) **butter**
1/3 cup (75 mL) chopped **onion**
1/3 cup (75 mL) chopped **red and green sweet peppers**
1 cup (250 mL) fresh sliced **mushrooms**
1/3 cup (75 mL) cooked **wild rice**
1 cup (250 mL) cooked **long grain rice** (1/2 cup (125 mL) raw rice to
   1 cup (250 mL) chicken stock)
1/3 cup (75 mL) chopped **walnuts**
3/4–1 tsp (3–5 mL) **Worcestershire sauce**
Generous dashes of **tarragon, rosemary,** and **sweet basil**
   (approximately 1/4 tsp (1 mL) of each, or more, to taste
Salt and **pepper** to taste
1 Tbsp (15 mL) **lemon juice**
1 tsp (5 mL) **paprika**

* Rinse chicken in cold water. Pat dry. Carefully loosen skin. Set aside.
* Melt 2 Tbsp (25 mL) butter in a small skillet. Saute onion and pepper until
tender crisp. Add mushrooms and saute until limp. Remove from heat.
* Add cooked rices, walnuts, Worcestershire sauce, herbs, salt and pepper. Mix well.
Cool.
* Pack about 1/2 cup (125 mL) of stuffing between skin and flesh of chicken breast.
Place chicken in a baking dish.
* Melt remaining butter. Stir in lemon juice and paprika. Baste chicken generously
and frequently with this mixture.
* Bake uncovered in a 350°F (180°C) oven for 3/4–1 hour.

4 servings

Fresh Fruit Romanoff
with Blueberries and Peaches

Donna Laceby says, "this recipe is also fantastic with fresh sliced strawberries or raspberries."

1 cup (250 mL) **whipping cream**
1 cup (250 mL) quality **French vanilla ice cream** (Baxter's Carriage Trade)
2 Tbsp (25 mL) **Cointreau**
4 fresh **peaches**
1/2 cup (125 mL) fresh **blueberries**
2 tsp (10 mL) **grated orange rind** (optional)

* Whip cream in a food processor or with an electric mixer. Add ice cream and blend well. Stir in Cointreau and blend again.
* Cover and chill.
* Prepare fruit just before serving. Wash blueberries and peaches. Slice peaches. Combine fruit and place in individual serving dishes.
* Whip cream sauce with a whisk. Pour 1/2 cup (125 mL) over each serving. Sprinkle a little orange rind on top if desired.

4 servings

Balmoral Motel
Tatamagouche

Looks are deceiving at the Mill Room, of the Balmoral Motel. Although the view of the Waugh River is pretty, the decor is typically motel nondescript-orange Western style furnishings and background twangy bass muzak. But shown the menu, you will be surprised. Shown the food, you will be amazed.

Imagine a motel dining room that serves delicately smoked trout graced with sweet garden tomatoes, buttered toast and a dab of horseradish. The bread basket overflows with European sour dough rye bread, homemade white bread and baking powder biscuits. The main entree platter is so full you cannot see the china. It is covered with side dishes like sweet and sour red cabbage, steamed whole potatoes, cucumbers in white sauce, numerous pickles and relishes. Whether you have schnitzel, goulash, or kasseler rippespeer, you are in for some hearty old fashioned German cooking.

Mr. and Mrs. Adolf Hoetten came to Canada in 1979 from their home town of Hammlerwald, Germany. They had a good business selling restaurant machines, but were hoping to leave behind their stressful, hectic lifestyle. They bought the Balmoral Motel originally as an investment, but soon found themselves actively involved in the running of the motel and restaurant.

Finding what Mrs. Hoetten describes as 'fast food' being served out of the large commercial kitchen, she slowly introduced a few German dishes into the menu. She made up small batches so that her family could eat up food that would not sell. The first dish she experimented with was rouladen, a rolled beef steak fried with spices, bacon and onion. She made up six portions and waited three days for an adventurous soul to try one. Then a local shoe store owner ordered the dish. He liked it and started recommending the rouladen along with his footwear. Today many of Mrs. Hoetten's diners are local people who tell her they appreciate her cooking because it is 'different'.

Mrs. Hoetten sees a difference between her European cooking and that of her Canadian neighbours. She tends to use more spices and her food preparation is more time consuming. Cooking German style food while living in Tatamagouche takes some planning. Ingredients Mrs. Hoetten could count on at home are not readily available here. She travels to Halifax for spices, but has relatives mail her nutmeg flower blossoms and tapioca glaze from Germany. The Kirschwasser (cherry brandy) which blesses her Black Forest Cake is also imported specially because the Austrian brand she prefers cannot be purchased here. She says, 'Austrians make the best Kirschwasser'.

For German sausage and sauerkraut, the Hoettens have only to travel to Truro, where their German butcher also smokes the pork for the kasseler rippespeer. They can also order fine sausage from Montreal where there is a large German population.

The Hoettens miss certain old country vegetables. They have encouraged a local farmer to grow leeks, kohlrabi and white asparagus for them. The kohlrabi has a delicious bulbous cabbage flavoured stem which Mrs. Hoetten likes to steam in strips and serve with white sauce or meat stuffing. She bakes the leeks or makes them into soup. The asparagus which are white because they are shielded from sunlight are not yet on the menu. Mrs. Hoetten is hoping to add them when the asparagus beds are developed enough to provide her with a plentiful supply.

A mainstay of the dining room is the sourdough rye, which Mrs. Hoetten likes to have *'in the breadbasket all the time'*. She makes it herself in the winter, but a German farmer in New Brunswick bakes it for her in the busier months. Mrs. Hoetten notes that the temperature of the water and flour have to be *'just right'* for the sourdough to work properly. A trick she uses to ensure a good crust is to place a cup of water, which fills the oven with steam, next to the baking bread.

But without a doubt the highlight of the menu is the smoked fish. The process is a hot smoke that cooks and smokes the fish at the same time. It differs from the usual cold smoke, which makes a salty firm product. This fish has a freshly cooked open fire flavour. The Hoettens smoke trout, mackerel, salmon, sea bass, eel and local white fleshed fish. Although they brought the smoker with them from Germany for family use, lucky diners at the Mill Room can now share this delectable dish with them.

Curry Schnitzel

The banana and curry flavours blend together beautifully in this dish. Use any fresh, canned, or dried fruit you fancy.

1 lb (454 g) **pork cutlets**
1/2 cup (125 mL) and 1 tsp (5 mL) **white flour**
2 beaten **eggs**
1 cup (250 mL) **dry bread crumbs**
1/4 cup (50 mL) **shortening**
1 tsp (5 mL) **butter**
1/2 ripe **banana**
1/4 cup (50 mL) **beef stock**
1/4 cup (50 mL) **light cream**
1/4 tsp (1 mL) or more **curry powder**
2 fresh sliced **peaches** or 1–14 oz (398 mL) can peaches
Salt and **pepper** to taste

* Trim meat and slice it as thinly as possible. Tenderize by pounding with a meat mallet or the edge of a plate.
* Dredge in 1/2 cups (125 mL) flour. Dip in egg, then in bread crumbs. To set coating, place on a cooling rack for a few minutes.
* Melt shortening in a heavy skillet. Brown both sides of meat over medium-high heat. Remove to a baking dish. To cook pork thoroughly, place in a 325°F (160°C) oven for 10–15 minutes, depending on the thickness of the meat.
* Melt butter in the same skillet used for the meat. Stir in 1 tsp (5 mL) flour and the sliced banana. Cook over low heat until banana is soft.
* Whisk in cream, stock, curry powder, salt and pepper.
* Add fresh or drained, canned peaches. Cook a few minutes to heat the fruit.
* Serve immediately, pouring the sauce over the hot, crispy meat.

2–3 servings

Black Forest Cake with Cranberries

This authentic German recipe calls for little chocolate and no shortening. Mrs. Hoetten imaginatively substitutes Nova Scotia cranberries for sour cherries, with delicious results.

4 **eggs**, separated
2 Tbsp (25 mL) warm **water**
3/4 cup (175 mL) **white sugar**
1 Tbsp (15 mL) **vanilla**
3/4 cup (175 mL) sifted **cake flour**
1/2 cup (125 mL) **cornstarch**
3 Tbsp (50 mL) **cocoa**
2 tsp (10 mL) **baking powder**
Grated **peel** and **juice** of one **lemon**
3 cups (750 mL) whole **cranberry sauce**
3 cups (750 mL) **whipping cream**
6 Tbsp (75 mL) **Kirschwasser**
1 oz (28 g) square **semi-sweet baking chocolate**

* Line the bottom of a 10" (25 cm) springform pan with waxed paper. Butter the paper.
* Beat egg whites until stiff. Place egg yolks, water, and sugar in a large bowl. Beat for 1 minute at high speed until creamy and light.
* Sift together: flour, cornstarch, cocoa and baking powder.
* Gently fold egg whites, lemon juice, grated peel, vanilla, and flour mixture into beaten egg yolks.
* Pour into springform pan. Bake in 375°F (190°C) oven for 25 minutes. Remove from oven and let sit 5 minutes. Run a knife around edge of pan and remove sides. Peel off wax paper and place cake on cooling rack.
* When cake is completely cooled, slice into 3 layers with a serrated knife. Place bottom layer on serving plate.
* Whip cream. Set aside 1/2 cup (125 mL) of whole cranberries to garnish the top.
* Sprinkle 2 Tbsp (25 mL) Kirschwasser on the bottom cake layer. Spread 1 1/4 cups (300 mL) cranberry sauce on the layer, followed by one quarter of the whipped cream.
* Place the middle layer on the cake and repeat the fillings of Kirschwasser, cranberry sauce, and whipped cream.
* Place the top layer on the cake. Sprinkle with remaining Kirschwasser. Spread the rest of the whipped cream on the top and sides of the cake. Grate chocolate and sprinkle on the cake. Garnish the top with a circle of cranberries.
* Refrigerate at least one hour, but it is best to allow the cake to mellow overnight.

8 servings

The Blomidon Inn
Wolfville

Gale Hastings says she finds it hard to talk about the Blomidon Inn dining room apart from the inn itself. To her, they are one concept. This is lucky for the people who come to the Blomidon Inn merely to dine. They are given the same special treatment afforded the overnight guests.

The Blomidon Inn is a stately Victorian mansion. It is situated (as the pamphlet states), *'on two and a half acres of terraced lawns shaded by century old elms, chestnuts and maples'*. People don't just see the sign and drop in for a bite. As Gale says, *'it takes a commitment to drive up the driveway, walk up the granite stairs, past the weeping cherries and through the heavy mahogany door'*. Inside the front door, on the right is the *Rose Room*. The *Blue Room* is on the left. Straight ahead, an ornate staircase sweeps upstairs.

Gale and Peter Hastings bought this large imposing residence at a tax sale. In a century, it had evolved from a sea captain's mansion to a hotel with a checkered reputation. During the 1960s Acadia University renovated it as a girls' residence. Once during the history of the house, Gale's mother owned it, and Gale and Peter were married there.

When the house came up for sale the Hastings had already owned and restored eight other homes. They bought it with their eyes open. Gale says they felt the house *'deserved better'*. They decided the difference in effort between doing a mediocre and a proper restoration job on the house was minimal. So they decided to "go for the best".

Gale says expectations of visitors are high because the building is so *'grand'*. But the Victorian analogy stops here. Although the house may look formal, it is owned by two young people whose attitude to innkeeping is very much 20th century. If one looks beyond the plaster cornices, dados and marble fireplaces, one notices a relaxed country atmosphere. The rooms are decorated with pretty cotton prints. The dining room tables are covered with English rosebud china and napkins Gale has sewn herself.

While Peter manages the business, the kitchen is Gale's domain. She says she started serving meals as a service to her guests. She hated to ask them to leave a cozy game of Scrabble by the fire, to seek sustenance elsewhere. Today the Blomidon dining room serves fifty to one hundred dinners in an evening, and not only to overnight guests. It has become a *'special event'* place for many local people.

The inn was open seventeen months before Gale, who is a teacher by profession, stepped into another commercial kitchen. Although she says she doesn't know the

names of restaurant kitchen equipment, she has a natural talent for food preparation. Her sense of visual presentation is exquisite. The bread basket is a good example. Filled with Gale's grandmother's oatmeal bread, delicate cheese wafers and traditional oatcakes, it is topped with a beautiful contrasting touch — a twig of red cherries. Another example is the chicken Elizabeth, a stuffed chicken breast enclosed in a beautiful braided pastry.

The Blomidon Inn menu offers such Nova Scotian specialties as Willy Krauch salmon, Solomon Gundy, Digby scallops and Annapolis Valley fruit desserts. It reflects Gale's attitude to food service. She tries to give people what they anticipate eating in a Maritime country inn. She aims to please, and service is an important part of the operation.

The Blomidon kitchen has a system for delivering food in optimum condition. Dining room guests are staggered four, every fifteen minutes. An order board above the counter tells the cook what orders are coming up. But it is the waitress who helps the cook pace the meal by observing the timing of the diners. Gale likes to serve food that is *piping hot'*.

The kitchen itself looks like a relic from an *Upstairs/Downstairs* set. Gale looks forward to gutting it. She will design her new kitchen around the menu, rather than vice-versa. In the meantime, no one is complaining about the cookery out of the present kitchen — quite the contrary.

Apple Gruyère Tart

Gale Hastings serves these tarts as appetizers, on a platter surrounded with apple slices, cheese tidbits and walnuts.

Tart shells
— Your favourite pastry recipe. A 9" (22.86 cm) double crust recipe will yield 24 small tarts baked in muffin tins— **wax paper** and **rice** for baking

Filling
2 Tbsp (25 mL) **unsalted butter**
5 **scallions**
2 **apples**
1/4 tsp (1 mL) freshly grated **nutmeg**
1/8 tsp (1/2 mL) **curry powder**
3/4 lb (340 g) **Gruyère cheese**
1 cup (250 mL) **whipping cream**
3 **eggs**
3 Tbsp (50 mL) **dry vermouth**
salt and **pepper** to taste

The tarts are prebaked as they will get soggy if the moist filling is put in the uncooked dough. The rice and wax paper help the tarts maintain their shape.

* Roll out pastry and cut circles to line the muffin cups.
* Line the dough with wax paper which conforms to the cup shape and extends 1" (2.5 cm) above the rim.
* Fill each lined shell with rice up to the rim.
* Bake 10 minutes in a 425°F (220°C) oven. Remove from oven and carefully remove wax paper and rice. Discard.
* Prick pastry to allow steam to escape. Return to oven for 5 more minutes.
* Chop scallions. Peel, core and chop apples.
* Melt butter in a stainless steel pan. Saute scallions, apples, nutmeg and curry powder until apples are soft.
* Combine eggs, cream, vermouth, salt and pepper.
* Grate cheese.
* Fill the tarts with a layer of apple mixture, then cheese, then egg mixture.
* Bake in a 375°F (190°C) oven for 25 minutes until puffed and golden.

Yields 24 small tarts

Chilled Strawberry Soup

Wonderful on a hot summer's day! The Blomidon Inn serves other chilled soups such as raspberry, blueberry, peach and apple curry.

4 cups (1 L) mashed **strawberries**, either fresh or frozen and defrosted
1 cup (250 mL) **white sugar**
1 cup (250 mL) **sour cream**
4 cups (1 L) **ice water**
1 cup (250 mL) **dry red wine**
1/8–1/4 tsp (1/2–1 mL) fresh grated **nutmeg**

* Blend all ingredients. Chill. Garnish each serving with a strawberry fan and a mint leaf.

4–6 servings

Chilled Scallops in Green Mayonnaise

If you like raw scallops, try marinating them overnight in the vermouth, rather than cooking them.

1/2 cup (125 mL) **dry vermouth**
1/2 **bay leaf**
2 springs fresh **parsley**
1 lb (454 g) **scallops**
1/2 cup (125 mL) homemade **mayonnaise**
1/3 cup (75 mL) fresh finely chopped **greens** (any combination of green onions, parsley, spinach, swiss chard, dill)
salt and **pepper** to taste

* Place vermouth, bay leaf, and parsley in a medium-sized saucepan over medium-high heat. Bring to a boil.
* Stir in scallops and reduce heat to simmer. Remove scallops when they are opaque (almost immediately, do not overcook). Reserve cooking liquid, discarding bay leaf and parsley.
* Blend: mayonnaise, greens, salt and pepper.
* Add scallops to mayonnaise. Thin with a few tablespoons (30 mL) of cooking liquid.
* Marinate in the refrigerator for 4 hours. Serve on a bed of greens and garnish with lemon wedges and sprigs of dill or parsley.

As an appetizer, serves 6

The Bright House
Sherbrooke

The historic Bright House was built in 1850. It was owned first by the Cameron family, and later a clan of MacKeens. But when Geoffrey Turnbull bought the house in 1974, it must have been the name of the third owner, Arnold Bright, that captured his imagination.

With the help of friends, family and local craftsmen, he converted the two front parlors into a restaurant dining room. The woodwork was fastidiously scraped. Lemon yellow paint was applied to some floors. The rooms were decorated, transforming the house into a warm *'bright'* home.

In the same spirit, the outside clapboards were painted colonial yellow. A moss green roof was applied and ferns were planted, softening the bottom edges of the house. Inside the main dining room there were no curtains on the windows, lest they deter even one ray of sunshine from entering in.

The Bright House started serving meals in 1975. When Geoffrey Turnbull left a few years later, to produce current affairs programs at CBC, his parents, Wynneth and Gordon Turnbull took over management of the restaurant. Mrs. Turnbull is in charge of the kitchen and Mr. Turnbull seems to be in charge of keeping up everyone's spirits. He says that in the division of labour between them, *'she does the dirty work'* and *'I get to eat the good food'*. Geoffrey gets together with his parents in the winter *'to plan things'*, and costing is a collective family activity.

Mrs. Turnbull describes Bright House fare as *'typically English old country food'*. Traditional favourites include roast beef with Yorkshire pudding, and steak and kidney pie, billed as *'the Country Meal of England'*. They also serve a sherry nutmeg cake which is gorgeous. To enhance the English flavour of the food, the walls of the dining room are decorated with old lithographs of His Royal Highness Prince Albert and Hastings.

This is not to overemphasize the Englishness of the place, for although Mrs. Turnbull grew up in Northern England, her husband Gordon can be heard answering the phone *'top o' the morning'*. Gordon, also known as Scottie, and a member of the Black Watch says that he travelled all over Nova Scotia without seeing a single kilt, so he donned his Turnbull tartan. This is much to the delight of the diners.

Last year two widowed sisters came through on a bus tour. Not long after, Gordon received a package in the mail from them. It contained their great grandmother's sterling silver cairngorm (shoulder pin), bonnet badge, shawl holder and skein dhu (stocking knife). As childless women, they were passing their heirlooms to an appreciative Scot.

The kitchen in the back of the Bright House is small, but efficiently designed with commercial kitchen equipment and a pretty quarry tile floor. Many of the items on the menu, including the popular seafood casserole are served pot pie style. Mrs. Turnbull prepares large bowls of the mixtures (such as the casserole with scallops, sole, and lobster in sherry sauce) and keeps them chilled in the fridge. Close by, in the freezer, are the individually wrapped pie crusts. Other commercial equipment includes a dry steam pressure cooker, which cooks vegetables and poaches fish in minutes, and two microwave ovens.

Just behind the house is a garden where peas, beans, lettuce and other vegetables are grown to feed Bright House guests. Mrs. Turnbull prefers not to use canned vegetables, and supplements her own home grown vegetables with sugar peas and beans from her neighbour Leita Aulenback. A woman in her eighties, Mrs. Aulenback also picks wild blueberries and grows rhubarb for Bright House pies.

A bakery was recently built in the Bright House back yard and it is a perfect complement to the restaurant. It turns out wonderful breads, cinnamon buns, rolls, scones and pies. The fresh baking adds much to the menu. The herb bread marries well with the house paté; the whole wheat bread is perfect for soaking up the baked beans and smokies *(recipe included)*.

Fourteen women from nearby Ecum Secum work at the Bright House. They wear self-sewn period costumes. Mr. Turnbull says that the *'girls'* work together *'like a family'*. Heading the family is Mrs. Turnbull, whom they call *'mother'*. Maybe this homey feeling rubs off on the eating guests. The warmth of the Bright House radiates from somewhere beyond the yellow pine boards and the sun streaming in the windows.

Smokies

This is a dish of wonderful contrasts — the salty, smokey fish, with the sweet, rich cream and the juicy tomato. Serve it with buttered whole wheat or rye bread. It's great for dipping.

4 – 2" (5 cm) pieces of **smoked mackerel, haddock, or cod**
1 large **tomato**
1 cup (250 mL) or more, **whipping cream**
paprika

* Butter 4 custard cups. Skin and bone smoked fish. Slice tomato.
* Place in each cup: a slice of tomato, a piece of fish and whipping cream to cover.
* Sprinkle with paprika and bake at 350°F (180°C) for 15 minutes, or until bubbly.

4 servings

Steak and Kidney Pie

This dish is listed in the Bright House menu as the country meal of England. *If you prefer less kidney flavour, blanch it by placing it in a large pot of cold water. Bring it slowly to a boil and then reduce the heat. Simmer until cooked through. Remove it from the water, pat dry, and proceed with the recipe.*

3 Tbsp (50 mL) **shortening**
1 lb (454 g) **round steak**
1 lb (454 g) **beef kidney**
1 large **onion**
1 cup (250 mL) sliced fresh **mushrooms** or 1-10 oz (284 mL) can mushrooms
1/4 tsp (1 mL) **ginger**
1/4 tsp (1 mL) **dry mustard**
1/4 tsp (1 mL) **pepper**
1/2 tsp (2 mL) **salt**
1/2 tsp (2 mL) **Kitchen Bouquet** (optional)
1 cup (250 mL) or more **water, stock** or **canned mushroom liquid**
Pastry for a large single crust pie

* Trim membrane and fat from kidney. Cut steak and kidney into 1/2" (1.25 cm) cubes.
* Melt 2 Tbsp (25 mL) shortening in a large skillet. Brown meat over medium-high heat. Remove meat and juices from pan.
* In same pan, melt 1 Tbsp (15 mL) shortening. Chop onion and saute until translucent. Add mushrooms and saute a few more minutes.
* Combine all ingredients and pour into a greased casserole (10"x10"x3") (25 cm x 25 cm x 7.5 cm) or a large pie plate. Seal with aluminum foil. Bake at 250°F (120°C) for 2-3 hours until tender. Add more liquid if necessary.
* Meanwhile prepare and roll out pastry. After removing casserole from oven, cool slightly and gently cover with pastry.
* Bake at 425°F (220°C) for 10-15 minutes until nicely browned.

4 servings

The Cape House Inn

Mahone Bay

Twice a year, Ray and Ann Caverzan move house. In the spring their living room furniture is shifted into the sitting room. To fill the empty space, nine dining room tables and forty chairs reappear after a sleepy winter in the shed. In the kitchen, the wood cook stove is unhooked and put in the corner. And the small pots and pans are retired to an upper shelf as the large commercial ones are pressed into service.

Each summer and fall the Caverzans share their interesting home with the eating public. Perched on a hill overlooking the town of Mahone Bay, their house is a two-hundred-year-old colonial red, Cape Cod. Guests enter through the back way, amid details of rural domestic order; beautifully kept lawns and flower beds, piles of split and neatly stacked firewood, red petunias spilling out of graying wooden crates. Passing by the shed, an open door reveals restaurant activity — Ray's fish filleting bench, bushels of fresh tomatoes.

The inside of the house is also meticulously cared for. The woodwork has been scraped down and oiled, the brass polished. Paint, paper and fabric have been applied with care and imagination. Great travellers, the Caverzans decorated their rooms with treasures gathered from all over the world; everything from antique clocks to wrought iron to folk art.

The Cape House Inn menu also reflects the lifestyle and food interests of the owner/chefs. Ann says, *'we cook what we like to eat'*. Travelling during the winter, they pick up ideas for dishes to serve at home in their own restaurant. And so the menu evolves from year to year.

The Caverzans like to serve dishes that are *'different'*. The bread basket comes filled with Ray's crisp croissants instead of the obligatory roll. Creamed scallops are served in unique individual scallop-pastry shells. Another specialty of the Cape House is lobster cardinal, in which the lobster meat is flambéed in brandy and served in a secret cardinal red sauce.

However, not all dishes served are of an international flavour. Traditional Nova Scotia favourites included in the menu are haddock chowder, Willy Krauch smoked salmon, and kedgeree, a casserole of fish, tomatoes and rice. A Lunenburg County special is the country lunch which includes Lunenburg sausage, baked beans and sauerkraut.

The absence of a kitchen door makes for easy traffic flow for the waitresses. It also

means that diners can see into the kitchen. This is not a problem, for what the public sees is not institutional clutter, but the glow of another warmly lit pine room. The Cape House kitchen is as pretty as the rest of the house. Ann doesn't call it a commercial kitchen, but the ample space is carefully designed into work areas — a marble slab for Ray's pastries, a dinner preparation spot for Ann, another for cleanup.

The kitchen ceiling has been raised to squeeze in an office loft. Here, Ann spends time every day on the phone tracking down ingredients. She might get a hot tip on a fresh halibut that has just been brought into a local wharf. Halibut will appear on the menu that day. A windfall of raspberries will appear in a cream cake later. Sometimes Ann has to call to Halifax or further for live lobsters, or to Montreal for the phyllo dough, essential to the baklava.

As charming as the inside of the house is, a big drawing card for diners is the view from the front verandah. Two hundred years ago, Christian Ernst cleared the forest and placed this house at the top of the hill overlooking the harbour. It is clear he had more on his mind than mere survival.

Today, a diner can finish his chocolate torte and espresso sitting next to a potted cedar, and look down upon the twinkling lights of Mahone Bay, below. What could be more civilized!

Coquilles St. Jacques in Pastry

The Cape House Inn serves an interesting variation of creamed scallops. Mini pie crusts are baked in scallop shells and the warm filling is spooned in just before serving.

Pastry for a single crust pie and 4 **scallop shells**
1–1 1/4 lb (454–567 g) **scallops**
1 cup (250 mL) **dry white wine**
1/8 tsp (1/2 mL) chopped fresh **tarragon**
2 Tbsp (25 mL) **butter**
2 **shallots**
1/4 lb (113 g) fresh **mushrooms**
2 Tbsp (25 mL) **white flour**
1/4 cup (50 mL) **whipping cream**
2 Tbsp (25 mL) **brandy**
1/2 cup (125 mL) **Gruyère cheese**

* Roll out pastry. Cut into 4 squares.
* Fit pastry square over the shells, pastry extending beyond edges. Place another shell over pastry. Press gently. Remove top shell.
* Bake at 425°F (220°C) 5–10 minutes until golden.
* Gently poach scallops in wine and tarragon until opaque. Do not overcook. Drain, reserving 1/2 cup (125 mL) poaching liquid.
* Melt butter in a small skillet. Mince shallots and saute until golden. Slice mushrooms and saute 2–3 minutes.
* Stir in flour, cream, brandy and poaching liquid. When thickened add cheese until melted, then scallops.
* Spoon into warmed pastry shells and serve.

4 servings

Raspberry Cream Cake

1 1/2 cups (375 mL) **white flour**
1 cup (250 mL) **white sugar**
1 1/2 tsp (7 mL) **baking powder**
1/2 cup (125 mL) **butter**
1 **egg**
2 tsp (10 mL) **vanilla**
2 **egg yolks**
2 cups (500 mL) **sour cream**
3 cups (750 mL) fresh **raspberries**

* Sift flour, 1/2 cup (125 mL) sugar, and baking powder into a large bowl.
* Melt butter and stir into flour mixture.
* Beat egg and 1 tsp (5 mL) vanilla together and stir into flour mixture.
* Form into a ball and pat into buttered 10" (25 cm) springform pan.
* Whisk together egg yolks, sour cream, 1/2 cup (125 mL) sugar and 1 tsp (5 mL) vanilla.
* Spread raspberries over cake base. Top with sour cream mixture.
* Bake for 1 hour 10 minutes at 375°F (190°C). Cool and refrigerate at least 2 hours until firm.

8–10 servings

Evangeline Snack Bar
Grand Pré

Some people call the restaurant *'Miss Stirling's'*. Others call it *'that place in Grand Pré'*, or *'the restaurant next to the motel across from the grape farm'*. But a restaurant doesn't really need a sign when it has been serving fresh cherry pie in the same spot for thirty-five years.

The owner and proprietor of the Evangeline Snack Bar is Miss Marjorie Stirling. After earning a degree in dietetics from Mount Allison University she worked in a big city restaurant *'with chefs and fancy stuff'*. She didn't like it much and so returned to Wolfville. There she opened up her own snack bar close by her brother A.R. (Bob) Stirling's orchards in Grand Pré.

It is the relationship between the snack bar and nearby farms that makes it such a special place. Every summer the menu evolves as the fruit ripens. The season starts with strawberry pie followed by pies made with raspberries, cherries, August apples, peaches and more apples. Miss Stirling stews the berries with a little sugar and cornstarch on top of the stove, and pours them into baked pie shells. Whatever variety, Miss Stirling says to make a good pie *'you have to use plenty of fruit'*.

Miss Stirling knows her apples. The best advice she has for a novice baker making a first apple pie is *'to hold the sugar'*.

Although the Snack Bar starts turning out apple pies with the first summer apples (such as the Close variety), Miss Stirling prefers a good sour apple. Her favourite pie apple has always been Gravenstein. However, her mind is open in such matters. Last year she tried the new Paula Red variety and concluded that it was a superior apple.

Making apple pie to the satisfaction of Annapolis Valley residents is no mean feat. Last summer she secretly tested the Paula Red on a local expert — a retired gentleman who *'eats apple pie every day'*. He complimented her on her pie, commenting that it was so good, it had to be a Gravenstein pie. She did not correct him, but got a chuckle out of it.

There is a feeling of security in a place where things have remained relatively the same for 35 years. Miss Stirling comments, *'My strongest point is that I'm always here'*. The white naugahyde bar stools and booths are original equipment. So are the milkshake machines and fridges which Miss Stirling says work better than the new ones. A different generation of English royalty graces the bone china cups and saucers than did years ago, but the plate glass shelves in the front window are still full. And the tartans, jams, and other tourist trinkets vie for space with the diners, as always.

But a perceptive diner can take note of the natural evolution of the building, while enjoying a bowl of fish chowder (made the same way for three decades with lots of celery).

It is a classic example of Nova Scotia additive architecture. Over the years the confines of the original shop have expanded into the outside. The new area is defined by a plastic corrugated roof, indoor-outdoor carpet and picnic tables. Surrounding this is a wrought iron fence and gate (that clangs shut at 7 p.m. sharp every evening).

Outside the fence is a planting of begonias in gorgeous fluorescent shades of red, orange and yellow. Hidden behind a hanging bamboo curtain, in the back, is an addition to the gift shop. And to handle the overflow, picnic tables have worked their way up the side of the grassy hill, beyond the begonias.

Neither is the kitchen·a clearly defined space. It starts in a patchwork of three small rooms inside, but spills outside. A big commercial stove sits under the plastic roof, along with some serving dishes and a table or two of overflow trinkets.

Inside one room, a table is covered with chopped onions and celery, about to be added to chowder. Two gigantic vats of finished soup are cooling in a sink full of water, covered by a window screen. In another room, thirty pound pails of fresh cherries and sugar stand next to wooden butter boxes stacked to the ceiling, filled with Royal Albert and childrens' moccasins.

The woman rolling out pies started working for Miss Stirling as a young girl. Some of Miss Stirling's *'girls'* began as young as 10 years of age (before minimum age laws). They saved their money and went on to Acadia University, but came back to work on weekends *'just because they liked it'*. One girl became such a favourite that customers sent her postcards and gifts and asked for her years after she was gone.

Miss Stirling has had two generations of waitresses working for her. She's had the mother and she's had the daughter. She says that she'll be *'finished'* when the grandchildren come to work!

Scones

Miss Stirling is famous for these scones which are closer to cookies than biscuits.

2 cups (500 mL) **white flour**
1 Tbsp (15 mL) **baking powder**
1/2 tsp (2 mL) **salt**
1/4 cup (50 mL) **white sugar**
1/4 cup (50 mL) **butter** or **shortening**
2 **eggs**
1/3 cup (75 mL) **milk** or **light cream**

* Sift together flour, baking powder, salt and 2 Tbsp (25 mL) sugar. Cut in butter until it is the consistency of coarse meal.
* Break eggs into a small bowl. Reserve a little of the egg white to brush on scones later. Beat eggs until light. Stir in milk.
* Slowly add eggs to flour mixture to make a soft dough. Stir vigorously until it comes freely from the sides of the bowl.
* Roll out on a floured board to 1/2"–3/4" (1–2 cm) thickness. Cut into triangles and place on oiled cookie sheet. Brush with beaten egg white and sprinkle with 2 Tbsp (25 mL) sugar.
* Bake at 450°F (230°C) for 12–15 minutes.

Yield: 12–16 scones

Fresh Cherry Pie

4 cups (1 L) fresh pitted **cherries**
1 1/4 cups (300 mL) **white sugar**
2 Tbsp (25 mL) **cornstarch**
pastry for a large double crust pie

* Stir sugar into cherries. Leave overnight.
* Pour juice off cherries and into a small saucepan. Whisk cornstarch into juice.
Stir over medium heat until thickened and clear. Mix cherries and thickened juice.
* Roll out bottom pie crust and place in pie plate. Fill with cherry mixture. Top
with upper crust.
* Bake at 450°F (230°C) for 10 minutes. Reduce temperature to 350°F (180°C)
and bake 20–30 minutes, only until crust is baked.

Yield: one large pie

Garrison House Inn

Annapolis Royal

One of Anna Redgrave's fond childhood memories is of a summer boarding house that her grandmother operated in England. And so, having one of her own has always been a cherished possibility.

About eight Christmases ago, Anna and Patrick Redgrave, an attractive young Toronto couple were passing through Annapolis Royal. They saw a realtor's sign on a derelict old hotel across the street from historic Fort Anne. Anna couldn't resist the opportunity to turn her romantic notion into reality. So she bought the place, and told her husband about her purchase back in Toronto.

Soon both Redgraves were busy preparing for the move to Annapolis Royal and the gargantuan task that awaited them — the transformation of the 130-year-old former Temperance Hotel.

This couple were well suited to the task. No formal apprenticeship could have prepared them better than the route they had already taken. Anna had studied interior design, worked in restaurants and even designed several. Patrick had a business background and a career as a wine importer. As a restaurant entrepreneur, he had opened Canada's first wine bar — *Vines* — in Toronto. Together, Anna and Patrick had bought, renovated and sold four houses. Along the way, they had learned plumbing, wiring and carpentry. With these skills, Anna, pregnant with daughter Alexandra, and a vision of a different life in the country, they set out. Their goal — to change the old hotel into the very special place it is today.

The Redgraves chose a name befitting the neighbourhood and honouring the 'the old boys', who are buried across the street in the Garrison cemetery. Despite the name, few parallels can be made between the inn and an army barracks!

The Garrison House is lovely. Anna has decorated the rooms to combine colonial elegance with English country charm. Pastel handloomed carpets thread their way up the main staircase. Crocheted lace curtains fill the sunny dining room windows. The dining room is actually two small rooms. The main one has eight tables. Another more private room is nestled behind the parlor. It is furnished with two small tables and one large drop leaf table with an upholstered love seat. It makes for very romantic dining.

Everywhere are shades of gray-blue, cranberry and forest green. Although the walls are covered with herb wreaths, art pieces and small printed wall paper, there is never a feeling of clutter or affectation — only an elegant, serene balance.

The same sense of balance runs through the menu at the Garrison House Inn. Neither pretentiously gourmet or self-consciously vegetarian, it offers choices. For example, the breakfast menu has something for everyone's eating style. The choice is granola and fresh blueberries, chocolate croissants, or standard bacon and eggs.

The dinner menu is thoughtful of travellers who might want a light meal. They can choose an iced gazpacho or borscht, a fresh herb omelette or a sorbet.

For diners in the mood for a rich celebratory dish, scallops are served in pernod and cream, lobsters with pasta, beef ragout in wine. There are also plenty of decadent desserts to choose from — cheesecakes and chocolate pot de creme for example.

People looking for more traditional Nova Scotia dishes will also be satisfied with the fish chowders, Digby scallops and Valley apple crisps.

The food is superb. Both Redgraves can be found in the kitchen at dinner time, and it is obvious that they care a great deal about the quality of the food they serve. They go to great lengths to acquire fresh ingredients, and then treat them with respect, never over-processing or overcooking them.

Annapolis Royal is situated on the very edge of the Annapolis Valley. Three days a week, Patrick or Anna will drive up as far as Bridgetown checking the stalls for fresh berries, peaches, apples and vegetables. They like to keep the menu flexible to accommodate what they find on these forages. And so their handwritten menu changes with the season.

Lobster with Snow Peas and Tarragon

2 cups (500 mL) fresh **snow peas**
2 Tbsp (25 mL) **olive oil**
1/2 cup (125 mL) finely chopped **onion**
10 fresh **tomatoes**
1/4 cup (50 mL) fresh chopped **tarragon** or 2 tsp (10 mL) dried tarragon
1 Tbsp (15 mL) **soy sauce**
1/4 tsp (1 mL) freshly ground **pepper**
1 cup (250 mL) **whipping cream**
2 cups (500 mL) freshly cooked, shelled, sliced **lobster meat**
Tabasco and **salt** to taste

* Steam peas until they turn bright green. Set aside.
* Heat olive oil in a dutch oven. Saute onion until translucent.
* Core and chop tomatoes. Add: tomatoes, tarragon, pepper and soy sauce to onions. Bring to a boil. Reduce heat and simmer, uncovered for 30 minutes.
* Remove from heat. Puree 3/4 of the tomato mixture. Pour into a bowl and add remaining tomato mixture.
* Wash the dutch oven. Pour in cream and place over medium heat until warm. Do not boil.
* Slowly add tomato mixture to cream, a few spoonfuls at a time, to avoid curdling.
* Add lobster. Stir over medium heat just until heated thoroughly. Add salt and tabasco to taste.
* Serve on fresh pasta topped with snow peas.

6–8 servings

Their fish comes out of the Fundy Shore from a fisherman who exclusively supplies the Garrison Inn. Their vegetables are also specially ordered. In March, the Redgraves call up a local farmer, with a list of vegetables and herbs they would like him to grow for them, for the upcoming season. Thus they are assured a supply of the leeks, fennel and other usually difficult to find things they like to cook.

On the Garrison House Inn brochure is a Latin phrase which the Redgraves believe captures the spirit of their adventure — *'Floreat Florebit'*. Anna translates it as, *'It flourished in the past and it shall flourish in the future'*. This phrase is well chosen because it aptly describes the transformation of the Garrison House Inn. But more than that, it captures the spirit of hospitality which Anna remembered and brought back to life.

Walnut and Apple Open-Face Sandwich

There are interesting textural differences in this upbeat grilled cheese sandwich —
the soft broiled apples, gooey cream cheese, chewy bread, raisins and nuts.

1 cup (250 mL) **cream cheese**
1/4 tsp (1 mL) **nutmeg**
1 tsp (5 mL) **cinnamon**
1/3 cup (75 mL) chopped **walnuts**
2 Tbsp (25 mL) **golden raisins**
4 slices hearty **whole-grain bread**
2 **apples**, crisp and crunchy, Granny Smith, Cortland or Gravenstein
2"x2"x4" (5 cm x 5 cm x 10 cm) piece of **old white cheddar cheese**

* Cream together: cream cheese, nutmeg, cinnamon, walnuts, and raisins
* Spread on bread. Top with wedges of cored *un*peeled apples.
* Slice cheddar cheese thinly and place on apples, 2–3 layers thick.
* Broil until melted and starting to brown. Slice on diagonal and serve.

4 servings

Gladee's Canteen
Hirtle's Beach

Flossie was the one who came up with the idea to open a small canteen on the beach. Just beyond the Hirtle family homestead, where Flossie, Gladee, Paul and Cyril grew up, is one of Nova Scotia's most spectacular combinations of sand, sky and water. The place is appropriately called — Hirtle's Beach. The family had managed with the farm and Dad's fishing, but Flossie thought a canteen might bring in some extra money. It might be fun, too!

1951 was the year they built the small shack right on the sand. It had a flip up door and an overhanging roof for the customers who stood outside. They christened it *The Seabreeze Canteen.*

There was no electricity then, so Paul and Gladee fried hot dogs and hamburgers on a two burner kerosene stove. They served them on rolls Gladee baked up at the house in her Lady Scotia wood range. For refrigeration they used the 18 inch thick chunks of ice they cut from Romkey's Pond during the winter. Stored in sawdust, the ice stayed frozen during the summer season.

Paul made homemade root beer in recycled beer bottles, and it was a hit! He dragged wash tubs of cold sea water up from the water's edge to keep the bottles chilled. Gladee remembers fondly how one of the *'loafers'* who hung around the canteen once leaned his chair back a bit too far. He found himself soaking in the root beer tub.

After a proper road was built and electricity found its way to The Seabreeze, things changed. The Lahave Dairy Truck could now make it down the road to deliver ice cream. Gladee started serving ice cream and homemade pies. And the outside world started beating a path to Hirtle's Beach.

In 1953, the Hirtles decided to expand not only the menu, but the building as well. They added on a dining room where people could eat inside, at long tables with benches. Gladee roasted chickens every day, and gained quite a reputation for her chickenburgers.

But the beach people really loved the french fries. On a busy day, the canteen would go through four, fifty pound pails of potatoes. John Hirtle, Gladee's father, peeled all those potatoes, and fresh potato fries remained on the menu until he died at age ninety-seven.

Flossie says that it wasn't unusual to see two hundred people on the beach on a Sunday afternoon in those days. They stayed open until 1:30 a.m. and Flossie and Gladee didn't get to bed until 2 or 3 in the morning. But they loved it.

In the summer of 1962, a kitchen was added to the back of the Seabreeze. But on October 7 that year, nature reclaimed her beach. Hurricane Daisy blew in the end of the canteen. Undaunted, the Hirtles dragged what remained of the kitchen up and over the edge of the rock beach, to a more secure spot. They constructed a new building, named it *'Gladee's Canteen'*, and it has remained relatively the same until the present.

Today Gladee and Cyril are in their late 70s. Paul has passed on and Flossie is eighty. But Gladee's Canteen is still a going concern. Flossie bakes all the barley bread and rolls, but now her daughter Mary and husband Eric Creaser do most of the cooking. Their daughter Wendy waits on tables. Their son Kevin washes all the dishes by hand alongside his grandmother. Cyril sweeps up at night.

Gladee's is a success today because of a new generation of good cooking. Eric, who is a mechanic in the winter, is *'fussy'* about the food he serves. The seafood must be fresh. The fish in the chowder must not be overcooked. The oil in the fryers must be changed often. All the haddock, scallops and lobsters used in the canteen are selected by Eric personally, from National Sea Products in nearby Riverport.

Behind the canteen is a large garden, which the family grows to supply the canteen with fresh beans, broccoli and swiss chard. The peas for Mary's fresh pea soup are picked off a trellis heavy with the Mammoth Melting Sugar variety, minutes before they are popped into the soup pot. All Mary's soups are made from scratch using garden vegetables, beef and chicken. She also makes the noodles for her chicken soup by hand with a rolling pin.

Every morning Eric and Mary roll out the pies together. On a busy weekend this could mean 25 pies. They make excellent fresh berry and rhubarb pies, but people come miles for the custard pies such as banana cream and coconut cream. Made with milk, butter and brown sugar, they are far superior to the commercial mix kind.

To explain why the food is so good at Gladee's, Eric says, *'We don't take short cuts. We make it like we would for ourselves'*. The recipes have evolved, he says with a chuckle, because *'people complain about the food and we keep working at it!'*

Flossie says that Gladee was always too shy to come out of the kitchen to meet people. But not Flossie. She loved to chat up the customers. And they appreciated her just as they appreciated the canteen. The Hirtles of remote Hirtle's Beach had something special and people found them. Proudly displayed on a wall in the canteen is Flossie's souvenir plate collection. They are all presents from visitors to Gladee's who have gone back home and sent her a memento from places like Massachusetts, Texas, Pittsburgh and Baddeck.

Recently, Kevin Creaser's artwork has decorated the dining room. Grandmother Flossie is proud of his photographs, and fish carvings. But she especially likes the drawing he did for the placemat — an illustrated history of Gladee's canteen. It gives expression to 30 years of effort by a fine Nova Scotian family. Not only have they put a tremendous amount of hard work into their endeavor, they have also put their hearts into it.

Sugar Pea Soup

A few times a week, Gladee likes to come down from the house to the canteen to have a bowl of Mary's sugar pea soup.

2 cups (500 mL) diced **carrots**
2 cups (500 mL) diced new **potatoes**
2 cups (500 mL) **water**
4 cups (1 L) flat Chinese **sugar peas**
2 cups (500 mL) **light cream** or **canned evaporated milk**
1/4 cup (50 mL) **butter**
1 Tbsp (15 mL) **sugar**
Salt and **pepper** to taste

* Place carrots, potatoes and water in a large pot. Bring to a boil. Reduce heat, cover and simmer until vegetables are soft.
* Add peas, cream, butter, sugar. Heat thoroughly over medium heat. Do not boil. Add salt and pepper to taste. Peas should be *'half crunchy'* when served.

4–6 servings

Barley Bread

The addition of barley flour makes the bread more dense, moist and chewy. You can buy the flour at a health food store, or grind pot barley in an electric coffee grinder, for an adequate substitute.

2 Tbsp (25 mL) and 1 tsp (5 mL) **white sugar**
2 Tbsp (25 mL) **dry yeast**
2 cups (500 mL) **warm water**
4 cups (1 L) **white flour**
1 cup (250 mL) **barley flour**
1 tsp (5 mL) **salt**
1 Tbsp (15 mL) **shortening**

* Dissolve 2 Tbsp (25 mL) sugar in water. Stir in yeast. Set aside until frothy (about 10 minutes).
* Sift together the flours, salt and 1 tsp (5 mL) sugar. Rub in 1 Tbsp (15 mL) shortening.
* Make a well in the flour. Pour in yeast water. Stir. Knead on a floured board until soft but not sticky.
* Cover with a damp cloth and place in a warm spot for 15 minutes.
* Knead again. Cover and allow to double in bulk.
* Punch down and shape into 4 balls. Grease 2 bread pans with remaining shortening. Place 2 balls in each pan, turning to grease all sides.
* Cover and allow to rise until almost double in bulk. Bake at 350°F (180°C) for 40 minutes until golden brown.

Yield — 2 small double loaves

Gramma's House

Port Saxon

Gramma's House doesn't really look much like the house that Gramma lived in until 1957, and Jean Turner visited as a child. The summer kitchen is gone off the back. The small Cape Cod rooms have given way to more modern spacious ones.

When Gramma died the property went out of the family for the first time since 1760 when the land in Port Saxon was granted to Solomon Smith. The new owners did more to renovate rather than restore the house. Later when Jean and her husband bought the house and brought it back into the Smith family, they added their own personalities to the old building. They added a deck, sliding glass doors and other modern adaptations.

Although paint, glass and wood altered the physical structure, it remained *Gramma's House* to the family that cared about it. When it came time to legally register a name for Jean's business, the Turner family wracked their brains. Jean says they asked each other *'What are we going to call Gramma's House?'*. Soon, the obvious name became evident.

Jean Turner's attachment to Gramma's House is understandable. She was born in the house. When she first opened her tea room in July of 1981, the invited guests included not only her parents, and an aunt from Boston, but also Flossie Perry from N.W. Harbour, the midwife who delivered her.

Jean Turner's cooking style can be best described by her statement, *'I do not own a cook book.'* But someone who has inherited Gramma Smith's recipe box wouldn't need one! However, Jean has not led a culinary sheltered life. Living most of her married life in Wolfville with her professor husband, she has had two careers herself, as nurse and teacher. But having travelled extensively, she has come back to what she knows best.

Jean feels that when people come to eat in her Port Saxon dining room *'they want the kind of food like is grown, cooked and eaten by people in this area.'* This means that the haddock is not cooked in wine and fancy herbs, but oven baked in light white sauce and served simply with salt and pepper and a baked potato. The fish comes to the kitchen straight from the nets of a neighbour. Jean considers it a *'sacrilege to freeze fish'* with the ocean a few hundred feet from her door.

Gramma's House brochure advertises *'19th century recipes'*. Some of the traditional dishes that Jean serves are the Indian and bread puddings, buttermilk pie, and a vinegar pie which is tangy and similar to lemon meringue pie. A favourite summer dish is hodge podge, a medley of baby vegetables fresh from the Turner garden. The dessert menu 'runs with the season' including whatever berries are available. Neighbourhood children have discovered a way to earn pocket money and appear at Jean's door, their arms laden with wild berries.

With the small dining room and a few overnight guests, Jean seems content. She cooks on a regular stove with small pots and pans. She has no desire to expand her business or menu to emulate larger institutional cooking styles.

It is obvious that Jean Turner enjoys what she does. Last Thanksgiving she served her traditional turkey dinner six times to a total of one hundred and ninety people. She decorated with candles and cornucopia. The dinners must have proved memorable to a number of local people because they have requested a rerun of this 'food event'.

After interesting years away, Jean Turner has found her way home. She enjoys the same beautiful view and clear sweet well water that many generations of her family have in the past. The people who enjoy her cooking and hospitality are glad that she did.

Hodge Podge

Jean Turner says that hodge podge is the way to celebrate the first new baby vegetables of the season. Amounts are approximate and other new vegetables may be used. Add them in order of required cooking time.

1 cup (250 mL) baby **carrots**
cold **water**
1/4 tsp (1 mL) **salt**
1 cup (250 mL) baby **string beans**
1 cup (250 mL) flat Chinese **sugar peas**
1 cup (250 mL) new **potatoes**
2 Tbsp (25 mL) **butter**
1/2 cup (125 mL) **light cream**
salt and **pepper** to taste

* Wash carrots and place in a large saucepan with water to cover and salt. Place on medium-high heat. Cover.
* Prepare beans. Wash and remove ends. Add to saucepan, cover and continue cooking.
* Prepare peas. Wash and string. Add to saucepan, cover and continue cooking.
* Prepare potatoes. Wash and dice. Add to saucepan, cover and continue cooking until fork tender.
* Drain vegetables. Add butter and cream and season with salt and pepper.

4 servings

Buttermilk Pie

Buttermilk is the liquid left after the butter curd is removed from cream. You can use purchased cultured buttermilk, or make your own in a food processor. Recipe follows.

4 **eggs**
1 cup (250 mL) **white sugar**
1/4 cup (50 mL) **white flour**
2 cups **buttermilk**
1/2 tsp (2 mL) **salt**
pinch of **nutmeg** or **mace**
pastry for a 9" (22.5 cm) pie

* Beat eggs. Add remaining ingredients, beating after each addition.
* Pour into unbaked pie crust. Bake at 375°F (190°C) for 45–50 minutes until the centre is firm.

To make butter and buttermilk:

4 cups (1 L) 32% **whipping cream**

* Pour cream into food processor fitted with plastic blade. Turn on and leave on until butter curds separate from the buttermilk (approximately 2–3 minutes).
* Pour off liquid buttermilk. Knead butter to remove excess liquid. Add 1/4 tsp (1 mL) salt if desired.

Yield 1 lb butter and 2 cups (500 mL) buttermilk

Harris' Seafood Restaurant
Dayton

Thirty years ago Charlie Harris had his own fishing boat and his wife Clara kept house for their young family. One day a friend from Connecticut, who loved Clara's cooking, offered to lend her some money to open up a restaurant. He said it was a sin that you couldn't get fish in a restaurant as good as Clara made at home. The rest is history.

Gesturing to the gymnasium sized restaurant whose name has become synonymous with Yarmouth and delicious seafood, Clara Harris says, *'I walked out of my house and into this!'*

They started out small in 1953 with a stove, a fridge and a table. They had so little room that Clara says they stored the soup pot under the table between servings. But the family was not afraid of hard work and long hours, so the business grew. A big break came when a local dance hall came up for sale. (It had originally been an air force barracks during World War II when the English fliers were trained at the East Camp near Yarmouth.) They continued working and the dance hall evolved into the Harris' Seafood on Doctor's Lake that people know today.

The building may be huge but there is a generosity about the furnishings, the service and the portions that wipes away any suggestion of emptiness. From the ceilings and walls hang fish nets, model boats, stuffed tuna, lobsters in plaster of paris, driftwood, buoys. You name it, and if you find it on a Nova Scotia beach, you'll also find it on the walls at Harris'!

Clara Harris has a great sense of visual showmanship. While sitting at one of the 25 or so tables, an individual diner can see many sights across the room — the gigantic red claws of a lobster at the next table, or a 5" high sailboat of meringue floating by on a piece of lemon pie. Blue shooting flames flaring from the Starboard Lounge are merely

the Maritime Brew in a preparatory stage. And birthday candles are a common sight. Harris' provides complimentary birthday cakes several times a week.

It goes without saying that Clara Harris cooks fish expertly. She says it is important to cook fish quickly at a high temperature. She keeps a small ruler in the kitchen and follows the old guide of cooking fish 10 minutes for each inch of thickness, in a 500–550°F oven. When frying fish in the restaurant, she uses only vegetable oil.

Still things are different from the days when Clara cooked only for her family and her friend from Connecticut. During an average season, Harris' Seafood Restaurant serves 25,000 meals a month. On a busy night it is not uncommon for them to prepare 365 dinners.

Now Clara's son, daughter and two other chefs do most of the cooking. The menu has expanded with the times to include fancier dishes like seafood crepes, seafood casserole with sherry sauce and beef stroganoff. But the quality is still maintained by Clara. She continues to put in sixteen hour days and looks twenty years younger than her age, for all her hard work. Clara says that not only does she supervise, she *'also answers all the foolish questions!'*

Charlie Harris remains in charge of buying and cutting the fish, the *'steamers'* (soft shelled clams) and the lobsters. If they are not up to his standard, he sends them back.

Clara's son-in-law who is an accountant and part time manager of the restaurant says Clara's secret of success if that *'she treats people special'*. He says that she'll be all dressed up in a pant suit, as hostess in the dining room, when someone asks for a dish that has not been on the menu for years. She rushes into the kitchen, puts on an apron and makes it. Clara says simply, *'If people fancy something, you should give it to them'*. People have been fancying Clara's cooking for over 30 years now.

Lobster Nova Scotia Style

This lobster and cream combination is simple to prepare, but delicious. You can easily double or triple the recipe. Serve with rice or mashed potatoes.

2 Tbsp (25 mL) **butter**
2 cups (500 mL) freshly cooked and shelled **lobster meat**
2 tsp (10 mL) **cider vinegar**
1 cup (250 mL) **whipping cream** or **light cream**
salt and **pepper** to taste

* Melt butter in a skillet. Add lobster meat and saute a few minutes.
* Stir in vinegar, then cream, salt and pepper. Heat through gently over medium low heat.

4 servings (1/2 cup lobster meat each)

Maritime Brew

To make this dramatic beverage requires some special equipment and a lot of nerve! You will need:

a large goblet type glass with a handle and a base
a can of Sterno
a flameproof ladle
pot holders

2 tsp (10 mL) **brown sugar**
1 oz (28 mL) **dark rum**
hot **coffee**
2–3 Tbsp (25–45 mL) **whipped cream**
1 oz (28 mL) **amaretto**

* Assemble all equipment and ingredients.
* Light sterno. Heat glass over flame with a back and forth motion, for a few seconds.
* Place sugar in the glass and heat a few seconds more.
* Pour in rum. Heat glass back and forth over sterno until rum ignites. Douse immediately with hot coffee. Spoon on whipped cream.
* Place amaretto in ladle over sterno until it ignites. Pour flaming amaretto over whipped cream.
* Wrap the glass in a cloth napkin and serve.

1 serving

MacLeod's Canteen
Green Bay

MacLeod's Canteen looks just like any other roadside canteen you may have seen in your travels throughout Nova Scotia — a small homemade building with a handpainted sign and a vertically sliding window to dispense ice cream and fries. Forced to stop at these places when there is nothing else in sight for 50 miles, you would like to *'discover'* a local genius for food in a completely unlikely spot. At MacLeod's you don't have to settle for preprocessed frozen and refried whatever. Have a bowl of gorgeous clam chowder, a slice of smoked salmon quiche, or a Lunenburg pudding sandwich. Or if you must have grease, have a piece of freshly caught haddock in batter.

This canteen is not just a stopping-off place. Situated on a dead end road beyond Petite Riviere and within a few feet of the crashing surf and sand of Green Bay, MacLeod's Canteen is packed with people who have gone out of their way to get there.

The reason is the MacLeod family, who have been taking care of local people and tourists for 50 years. Now in their eighties, Malcolm and Rhoda MacLeod started selling homemade ice cream in 1929 under a tarp on the beach, to supplement their Depression income. In those days it was against the law to sell ice cream on Sunday. So they served ice cream in a dish, with a homemade cookie and called it lunch!

Their only child, Miriam MacIntosh, grew up in the business. Ten years ago Miriam, a professional nurse and her husband Jack took over management of the canteen.

Miriam's culinary efforts can be described in the best sense of the expression *'home cooking'*. Every summer morning she takes the path from her nearby cottage down to the canteen. She takes down her dog-eared, handwritten recipe scribbler and proceeds to make seven different pies. Her recipes are favourites she has collected over the years from friends and staff. Many of her recipes including the popular Northumberland scones come from Shirley Cohrs. She worked at and contributed much to the canteen in recent years. Miriam says *'Shirley is an excellent cook with many creative ideas'*.

Miriam is open to new ideas and she says *'if someone comes along with a favourite recipe, we're glad to try it'*. One memorable example last summer was: *'Wik's dead Granny's pie'*. The recipe, as well as its name, were contributed by a local craftsperson. *'Everyone got a good laugh out of that one'*, she recalls.

After the pies are done, Miriam and her student helpers make scones, rolls and chowders in a kitchen which is smaller than most home kitchens. The delicious pies are rolled out on a two by two foot piece of formica counter. The dishes are washed by hand.

But Miriam says that with only four people cooking, serving and cleaning up, the kitchen need not be bigger or fancier. And the staff gets along extremely well. Miriam describes them as a *'happy, cheerful pleasant group'*, who are friends after working

hours. *'Often several children from one family work their school vacation until they move onto greater endeavours'.*

The only food not prepared on the spot is transported from the kitchen of neighbour Fran Van Schoewen. Her contributions are far from the standard fare of the average canteen — soups such as broccoli and leek, cabbage and bacon, cucumber and spicy chili.

Much of the success of the canteen can be attributed to local suppliers who are a loyal lot. Miriam describes Cecil Himmelman who supplies the fresh fish, clams and mussels from Bush Island as a *'genius'*. Fresh vegetables are delivered by a local farmer. And there is always an ample supply of wild blueberries, raspberries, blackberries and foxberries. Add a shortcake biscuit and Miriam's penchant for heavy cream — the results are irresistible.

MacLeod's Canteen is almost always packed. Older people come for an ice cream, to relax in the car and watch the water. Teenagers come for the pop and chips and each other. Tourists and those with more sophisticated palates come for the delicious food.

Still, the most popular item on the menu is fish and chips. People like to buy a cardboard trayful and wander down the beach amongst the sand, rock, wild roses and seagulls.

Green Bay and MacLeod's blend to make that magic summer combination of chips and sand, ice cream and sunshine.

Blueberry Shortcake

These shortcakes are special because of the combination of fresh and cooked berries. Prepare the biscuits and blueberry sauce in advance. Just before serving, whip the cream, stir in the fresh berries and assemble the shortcake.

Shortcake Biscuits

2 cups (500 mL) **white flour**
2 1/2 tsp (12 mL) **baking powder**
1/2 tsp (2 mL) **salt**
1 Tbsp (15 mL) **sugar**
4 Tbsp (50 mL) **cold butter**
1 cup (250 mL) **milk**

* Sift flour, baking powder, and salt into a bowl.
* Cut in butter until it resembles coarse meal. Quickly stir in milk until evenly moistened.
* Drop heaping tablespoonfuls onto an oiled cookie sheet. Bake at 450°F (230°C) for 10 minutes.

Yield: 12 biscuits

Blueberry Sauce

2 cups (500 mL) **blueberries**
3/4 cup (175 mL) **white sugar**
2 Tbsp (25 mL) **lemon juice**
1/4 cup (50 mL) **water**

* Blend together all ingredients in a saucepan over medium heat. Stew for a few minutes until berries change colour and sugar is dissolved. Do not cover and stir frequently.

To assemble Blueberry Shortcake

1 cup (250 mL) **whipping cream**
2 cups (500 mL) **fresh blueberries**
1 batch **blueberry sauce**
3 Tbsp (50 mL) **butter**
8 **shortcake biscuits**

* Whip cream. Stir fresh blueberries into sauce.
* Warm biscuits, split and butter. Place bottom layer on plate.
* Spoon over berries (approximately 2 Tbsp (25 mL) per serving).
* Add biscuit top. Spoon more berries (approximately 4 Tbsp (50 mL) per serving).
* Add a good dollop of whipped cream (approximately 1/4 cup (50 mL) per serving). Garnish with a few fresh berries.
* You can easily increase this recipe by adding up to 4 cups (1 L) more fresh berries to the sauce.

8 servings

Clam Chowder

This clam chowder is superb!

2 quarts (2 L) soft shelled **clams** in the shell
water
1 large **onion**
1/4 cup (50 mL) **butter**
3 **potatoes**
1-2 tsp (5-10 mL) **seafood seasoning**
2 cups (500 mL) **light cream**
salt and **pepper** to taste
sprigs of **parsley** (optional)

* Prepare clams by scrubbing them and changing the water several times.
* Place clams and 1/4 cup (50 mL) water in a large saucepan over medium-high heat. Cover and steam just until they open (5-10 minutes).
* Separate clam meat from shells, saving all broth from clams and saucepan. Set meat aside. Strain broth into a measuring cup. Add water, if necessary, to make 2 cups (500 mL) liquid.
* Peel and dice onion and potatoes. Melt butter in a large saucepan and saute onions until translucent. Add clam liquid, potatoes and seafood seasoning. Bring to a boil. Reduce heat, cover and simmer until potatoes are tender.
* Stir in clams (minced if you prefer), cream, salt and pepper. Heat gently. Do not boil. Serve with a sprig of parsley if desired.

6 servings

Marquis of Dufferin Lodge and Motel
Port Dufferin

When this old Cape Cod house was built 125 years ago, the parlor windows and Scotch dormers were positioned to look expectantly out to sea. From the perspective of Port Dufferin on Nova Scotia's Eastern Shore, the sea is not wild and woolly. The human habitations are not perilously perched on the edges of rocks. Rather, the shoreline forms a series of bays, coves, inlets and harbours. The towns are nestled securely into the lap of the land.

When the road came through, linking together the little villages along the shore, people looked up the road for mail, groceries and civilization. When outsiders started arriving by motor car, the day of the tourist home arrived. In the 1950s, the Cape Cod house became the Marquis of Dufferin Lodge and opened its doors to guests. In the 1960s a modern motel was added to the side of the lodge. The large picture windows focused on the road.

Michael and Eve Concannon came to Nova Scotia *'looking for a different pace'*. Originally from England, they had lived in Philadelphia where Michael was an aerospace engineer in *'the early exciting part of the space business'*. Eve was a teacher who ran her own school based on the English infant school. But they were ready for a change. They wanted to escape *'the heat of Philadelphia'*.

The view from the hill in Port Dufferin is serenity itself — the blue of Beaver Harbour is softly edge by thick forest green. Hardwood and Rocky Islands buffer the harshness of the open ocean and allow for excellent sailing on the harbour. The Marquis of Dufferin Lodge and Motel was up for sale. And so Eve and Michael (who calls himself a *'sailing buff'*) bought it.

The Concannons' basic attitude toward serving food to the public is simply to provide what people want. They have discovered that what people want is fish. So their menu is largely fish with a meat alternative.

The Eastern Shore is Willy Krauch land, famous for quality smoked fish. Michael says they were *'horrified to find that nobody was serving Willy's stuff around here'* As a result, Michael and his brother developed their own smoked salmon and smoked mackerel paté recipes for the restaurant. They used to be able to get salmon tails for the paté for free but Michael says they now have *'to fight for them!'*

In Port Dufferin, there is an ample supply of fresh scallops and white fleshed fishes such as flounder, haddock and halibut. The Concannons poach the fish gently in a little butter and lemon juice in the microwave. The scallops are pan fried. Michael says that not freezing them makes a big difference — *'there's a trick to cooking them — when they're fresh and just done, they shrink and go "POP" in the pan'*.

The Concannons insist on serving only fresh lobster. When it is in season they can look out the lodge windows to see the lobsters being unloaded at a nearby wharf. The supply is plentiful. Unfortunately the lobster season coincides with only 20 percent of the Concannons' tourist season. Michael expresses a frustration at this situation. This common problem has been aired all over the province by tourists who want the lobsters and restauranteurs who would like to please them.

Desserts at the Marquis of Dufferin range from typical English trifle, to crackers *'with a decent Canadian cheese'*. Eve says that it is important not to scrimp and use a cheap sherry in the trifle.

Although other parts of the house are due for renovations, it's easy to see where the Concannons' priorities lie. The front of the house which faces the water has recently been graced with a beautiful architecturally designed deck. A pretty glass sun porch with slate floors and Scandinavian pine was completed last year. It will be interesting to see how the Concannons transform the old Western style dining room to their own taste, in the future.

The beauty of Port Dufferin has a way of calming the nerves of the most harried travellers. Michael describes a *'metamorphosis'* that overcomes the tired motorist. A few hours after arriving he can be found in the dining room, finishing up a delicious fish dinner. Or else he can be found having a cup of tea outside on the deck, soaking up the fresh air and the green and blue shades of Beaver Harbour. It appears that the old Cape Cod has once again found people who appreciate its point of view.

Fresh Apple-Cranberry Relish

This relish freezes well. Eve Concannon sometimes adds horseradish to it as a delicious accompaniment to meat. She makes it in a food processor but it can be made in a blender, using smaller batches.

3 cups (750 mL) fresh **cranberries**
3 medium **apples**
2 medium **oranges**
1 cup (250 mL) **white sugar**
1/8 tsp (1/2 mL) **salt**
1/2 cup (125 mL) **walnut pieces**

* Wash fruit. Do not peel apples or oranges. Quarter and core apples. Quarter oranges and remove seeds. Cut apples and oranges into smaller pieces.
* Coarsely chop cranberries in a food processor with metal blade. Remove to large bowl.
* Coarsely chop oranges and apples together in food processor. Add to cranberries.
* Stir in: sugar, salt, walnuts.
* Make at least a day in advance. Store in refrigerator.

Yield: 4 cups (1 L)

Shandy

Michael Concannon says to make this shandy you need a 'proper English beer mug, the kind with the fish eyes, that is sold at Canadian Tire'.

1 1/2 cups (375 mL) **lemonade** or **ginger ale**
1 bottle Nova Scotia **beer** (*'any old kind will do'*)

* Fill mugs with equal amounts of lemonade or ginger ale, and beer. Always pour the lemonade or ginger ale first.

Yield: 2 drinks

Smoked Salmon Paté

This tasty paté calls for equal amounts of smoked salmon and cream cheese, which seem to go naturally together. You will need a food processor to make it.

8 oz (250 g) whole piece **smoked salmon**
1 small **onion**
8 oz (250 g) **Philadelphia cream cheese**
1/4 cup (50 mL) pitted **green olives**
2 Tbsp (25 mL) **anchovy fillets**
1 1/2 tsp (7 mL) **lemon juice**
1 1/2 tsp (7 mL) **worcestershire sauce**
1 1/2 tsp (7 mL) **horseradish**

* Soak salmon in cold water, in refrigerator, for 24 hours, to remove salt.
* Using metal blade process salmon and onion in food processor until onion is finely minced.
* Add remaining ingredients and process until consistency of peanut butter. Serve with an assortment of breads and crackers.

Yield: 2 1/2 cups (625 mL)

Mets Acadiens
Cheticamp

There is a narrow plateau of emerald green, arable land between the cliffs that plunge to the Gulf of St. Lawrence and the Cape Breton Highlands. The road that runs from Margaree Harbour to Petit Etang appears to cling to the cliff edge. So do the houses, whose gables have been cut off by their builders, so that the winter tempests will not sneak under the corners of the roofs and hurl them into the sea. This tells something of a people who, tenacious and inventive, have figured out a way to live in this beautiful, but challenging environment.

The French people of this area are descendents of the Acadians who, expelled from Grand Pré in 1756, escaped to Prince Edward Island. Fourteen families found their way back to Nova Scotia, but landed to the north on Cheticamp Island. They arrived with Anglicized names such as White (now changed back to LeBlanc) and O'Quinn (Aucoin), but today speak French and have much pride in their culture.

A grand example of this is the Co-operative Artisanale de Chéticamp Limitée. Mrs. Lucy Boudreau, manager of the Co-op says, *'the co-op was started in 1963 by a small group of women who hooked rugs, to work together to market their rugs, to improve their quality and to offer the customers a good price'*. They opened a small gift shop, staffed by volunteers. As the group grew and met with success, they decided to expand their horizons.

They opened up Musee Acadien and Mets Acadiens. Both museum and restaurant are dedicated to the preservation of the Acadian culture.

Mrs. Boudreau describes Mets Acadiens as a *very humble and homelike cafeteria*. Walking down the stairs into the restaurant is like walking into the kitchen of a co-op member. It is a large basement room with scrubbed linoleum floors, little card tables covered with red checkered plastic tablecloths and low fluorescent lighting.

The kitchen area is separated from the rest of the room by a formica covered counter. All food is prepared in this 8' x 12' space in full view of the diners. People lining up to place and pick up their orders can inspect the food on the spot. This system makes for a kind of relaxed chaos, but people on vacation likely won't find this a problem. The restaurant pamphlet states, *'seating capacity is limited but the wait would be well worth it'*.

While waiting, a visitor might look at the small museum, which is in an alcove at the end of the room. It features an ancienne chapelle, a spinning wheel, loom, churn and an assortment of artifacts gleaned from the community.

The specials du jour are posted in English and French, painted attractively on boards. Where else in Nova Scotia does a restaurant menu offer an exotic choice between *'smelts with tea or coffee'* (Diner aux eperlans) and *'blood pudding with a bun'* (sauce au boudin avec petit pain).

Mrs. Jeanne Bourgeois, who has been chief cook for ten years, says that the most popular dishes are the potato pancakes, the fricot (stews) and meat pies. She says that these foods are all enjoyed in Cheticamp homes today. Although the potato pancakes are served with sour cream in the restaurant (because tourists like it), they are eaten traditionally with molasses. The pancakes are made simply with grated raw potato (liquid drained), salt and flour and fried in lard.

Fish is a natural part of the local diet and the menu at Mets Acadiens. In addition to smelts, other fish dishes include *diner à la morue* (cod fish dinner) and fish chowder. This chowder differs from other Nova Scotia chowders as it has neither cream nor milk in it.

Recently the crab fishery has been added to more traditional fishery on this shore. The restaurant now offers the diner a crab sandwich and a crab salad.

Over the last twenty years, the efforts of the Co-operative Artisanale de Chéticamp Limitée have proved a success. They have helped make the name Chéticamp synonymous with quality hooked rugs. The Nova Scotia Museum acknowledges their work with an annual grant. They have helped preserve their traditions and have brought them alive to their children through demonstrations in the schools. Now it is time for their culinary efforts to be appreciated as well.

Chard, Légumes et Viande
Stewed Potatoes, Meat and Vegetables

4 **chicken drumsticks**
4 **chicken thighs**
1 cup (250 mL) **white flour**
2 Tbsp (25 mL) **butter**
1 Tbsp (15 mL) **oil**
1 large **onion**
8 cups (2 L) peeled chopped **potatoes**
boiling water
salt and **pepper**

* Cut chicken into small pieces, leaving bone in. Dredge in flour.
* Heat butter and oil in a large dutch oven. Brown chicken on both sides. Chop onion and add to chicken. Continue browning a few more minutes.
* Add potatoes and boiling water to cover. Bring to a boil. Reduce heat, cover and simmer for one hour or more, until tender. Season with salt and pepper to taste.

4–6 servings

Fricot à la Viande
Meat Fricot

This fricot is more like a soup than a stew. Add water during cooking, if necessary.

2 Tbsp (25 mL) **butter**
1 lb (454 g) **round steak**
1 large **onion**
1/4 cup (50 mL) snipped **chives**
8 cups (2 L) peeled chopped **potatoes**
boiling water
salt and **pepper**

* Cube steak. Melt butter in a large dutch oven. Brown meat.
* Dice onion and add to the meat. Continue browning for a few minutes.
* Add: chives, potatoes, boiling water to cover. Bring to a boil. Reduce heat, cover and simmer for one hour or more, until tender. Season with salt and pepper to taste.

4 servings

Milford House
South Milford

You can eat in the huge old-fashioned dining room at Milford House without staying the night. But chances are that after a full course meal you'll want to stroll down the wooded path to one of the cozy rustic cabins, light a fire and crawl into bed, or sit out on the porch and watch the sun go down over Home Lake. Another reason for wanting to sleep there is so you can have breakfast the next morning.

The dining room will be filled with enthusiastic young families enjoying themselves. More than likely all five highchairs will be pressed into service; the same highchairs that these young parents spilled food on as youngsters, as did the grandparents of the babies, back in the 1920s. In fact much of the Depression decor remains, from the peach-coloured glass vases of garden flowers to the moose head over the fireplace in the parlor.

Breakfast in the country is a special time, particularly for city folk who usually do not have the leisure time or the fresh air appetites to indulge. Warren Miller, the kindly manager with a twinkle in his eye, says, *'Why you wouldn't believe the amount of cooked cereal that goes out of our kitchen in the summer!'*

The hot mush is usually Red River Cereal (popular with the American guests who can't get it at home), or oatmeal porridge with a handful of All Bran thrown in. Another old standby is prunes, stewed in a little lemon juice. They are on the menu every day without fail. Add the other choices of homemade brown bread toast, bacon, ham, sausage, blueberry griddle cakes, french toast, eggs, juices, berries and conserves. You wish you had all morning to get through it. If that weren't enough, the Milford House pamphlet clearly states, *'Feel free to order seconds or larger portions'.*

The original house was built in the 1860s as the Thomas family home. Situated on the stagecoach route between Annapolis Royal and Liverpool, it soon became a regular stop for changing horses.

As the story goes, a group of travellers was forced by storm and blocked roads to spend a few days. It turned out these men were avid sportsmen. They convinced A.D. Thomas to build a log cabin on the lake behind the house, so that they might have a place to stay while they enjoyed the wilderness.

Over the years, up to two dozen cabins were built, and the place developed quite a clientele. Included in an early Milford House brochure was a list entitled "High Class

Guests", followed by the names of prominent people from Boston, Philadelphia and New York. High up the list was the name Dr. Edward Breck. He was a main character in Albert Bigelow Paine's 1908 camping classic *The Tent Dwellers*, set in the uncharted wilderness of *KedgeemaKoogee*. This year, one of the child guests of Milford House was the great-great grandson of *'Eddie'* Breck.

Another guest was a woman in her 60s from Philadelphia. She brought with her a faded photograph of herself and four other children in a canoe in 1930. And still another guest was *'Pit'* Longmire, who used to be a fishing guide at Milford House. Now 94, he drove from Granville Ferry for dinner.

The Milford House stayed in the Thomas family until 1968. That year a group of devoted guests purchased it with the idea of running it in the same simple way it had been for years. They asked Warren Miller, who knew the place better than anyone, to manage it. He started working for Mrs. Thomas in 1943 as a *'young fella'*, the only boy on a staff of 14 girls.

In summing up his over 40 year association, Mr. Miller says, *'Why I've had more fun....!'*. His children grew up at Milford House and now his grandchildren come to visit. His nine-year-old grandson likes to sit at the front desk and help out by telling guests that Grampy will be back soon.

Mr. Miller says that his staff is a *'good bunch'*. He doesn't worry about them at all. Since he doesn't believe in paying by the hour, people are paid on a weekly basis, and they can go home when their work is finished.

Mr. and Mrs. Miller eat dinner in the dining room every evening. Mr. Miller makes a point of going from table to table to say hello. Guests can count on a high spirited comment from their host as much as an overflowing bread basket.

When asked the secret of the Milford House kitchen, Mr. Miller replied, *'It's the plain home cooking, not all spiced up'*. *'Plain'* main courses include scallops, roast beef, turkey, duck, baked chicken, pork chops, haddock and poached salmon. These dishes are accompanied by generous portions of garden vegetables: mashed potatoes, beet greens, and corn on the cob. A choice of five desserts is not uncommon. Mr. Miller is right about the plainness of the food at Milford House — it's plain good.

Half Hour Pudding

This very old recipe is a sweet eggy version of corn meal mush, with a puffy crusty top. Milford House serves it hot with whipped cream, but you may prefer to eat it cold.

1 cup (250 mL) **corn meal**
4 cups (1 L) **cold water**
pinch **salt**
1/4 cup (50 mL) **butter**
1 1/2 cups (375 mL) **white sugar**
3 **eggs,** separated

* Place corn meal, water and salt in a heavy bottomed saucepan. Bring to a boil while stirring. Reduce heat, cover and simmer for 15 minutes.
* Remove from heat. Melt in butter and sugar. Cool.
* Beat egg white until stiff. Beat egg yolks and stir into corn meal.
* Fold in egg whites. Pour into a buttered square cake pan (8" x 8") (19.7 cm x 19.7 cm).
* Bake at 350°F (180°C) for a half hour (30–45 minutes) until firm.

8–10 servings

Steamed Marmalade Pudding

This recipe belonged to Annie Thomas, wife of A.D. Thomas who owned Milford House around the turn of the century. You may wish to add more marmalade to the batter, or use it as a garnish.

1 1/2 cups (375 mL) **ground suet**
1 cup (250 mL) **dry bread crumbs**
1 cup (250 mL) **brown sugar**
1/2 tsp (2 mL) **baking soda**
6 Tbsp (100 mL) **marmalade**
2 **eggs**

* Combine suet, crumbs, sugar and soda.
* Whisk together marmalade and eggs. Add to dry ingredients and blend well.
* Pour into a buttered 4 cup (1 L) pudding mold, or a bowl sealed with aluminum foil or wax paper and string.
* Steam for 3 hours. Serve with whipped cream or rum sauce.

8 servings

Normaway Inn
N.E. Margaree

Although David Macdonald, manager of the Normaway Inn says that *'people really come here for the scenery'*, he is only partly right. The Normaway has an excellent reputation for fine country food. It's true that few restaurants are surrounded by 250 acres of pastoral beauty, emerald mountains and trout springs. It's a fact that food is bound to taste better after a stroll down a pine-lined driveway in invigorating country air. It's also true that many of the people who eat at the Inn have come back after twenty or thirty years, and have wonderful childhood memories to soften their objectivity about the victuals. But a drive to the heart of the Cape Breton Highlands, down the mysteriously titled Egypt Road, to the Normaway dining room is well worth it, if only for the food.

When David Macdonald took over the management of the family business in 1976, he inherited over forty years of innkeeping tradition.

The Normaway was built in 1928 by a local boy, George *'Norman'* McPherson, who had gone away and made good. He left his home in Margaree with two aspirations — to come back rich, and to become a preacher. After making a fortune in gold in Colorado, he returned from Yonkers and built the Normaway as a summer retreat for clergymen. It was designed so that no two rooms would be adjacent.

The stock market crash of 1929 turned McPherson's fortunes around and the Normaway soon opened its doors to the public as an inn.

After World War II, John Macdonald, David's father, was fishing in the Margaree area when he heard that the Normaway was for sale. John and his brothers bought it. Their niece Marjorie married a local boy, Gerald Hart, and together they ran the inn for twenty-seven years.

When the Harts retired, and attempts to hire a manager to run the inn proved difficult, the Macdonalds decided to put the place up for sale. It was at this point in 1977 that David, then a student at St. Francis Xavier University, decided to try managing the inn for a year.

David approaches the inn with a respect for its past, but with ambitions for change. The dining room had always prepared home cooked meals, appreciated by city visitors. But David *'wanted to offer more than a one choice menu'*. He sought professional advice and was lucky to attract the services of John Wilson. This chef had worked in Canada and Europe and designed over twenty restaurants. John's mandate was to rethink the menu and set up a blueprint for the future kitchen and dining room.

The dining room that David inherited was originally the McPherson's three bay car garage. David comments that *'the width of the room is a testament to the length of the*

cars!'. The space has since been transformed into a pretty, although sparsely furnished room with hardwood floors, floral curtains and delicate blue and white china. The huge, small-paned windows look out on the gardens, fields and hills beyond.

John felt, that in the spirit of country cooking, the menu should be as simple as possible. The food should be prepared without heavy sauces, or commercial mixes which mask flavours. Wherever possible, natural fresh ingredients should be used.

The Normaway tradition has been for fine food prepared in a simple country way. David provides a menu that is 60% country dishes, such as barley soup and poached salmon. 20–30% is more sophisticated fare, including one gourmet dish per night, such as chicken with an orange sauce. The remaining 10% of the menu includes dishes unique to the Normaway. The fisherman's soup, a change from regular fish chowder was developed by David's sister Nora Fraser, especially for the dining room. It is made with tomatoes, fresh herbs and wine. Dessert choices range from sophisticated flans to chocolate brownies.

To provide country fresh food, all breads are baked in the Normaway kitchen. A large garden is grown to supply prime vegetables, as well as fresh dill, savory, basil and thyme which are used in the more complex recipes.

David believes that vegetables *'deserve extra attention'*. He employs an extra person in the kitchen for the two peak dinner hours, to ensure that they are properly steamed.

David Macdonald took over a seasonal business. But he has been doing his best to enhance the season, with Elderhostels, theatre nights and cross country ski clinics. He has also been building up a dining room with a reputation for fine food. Perhaps he is working towards a new definition of the term *'country food'*.

Tian of Zucchini, Spinach and Rice

3 lb (1.4 kg) **zucchini**
1/2 tsp (2 mL) **salt**
2 lb (900 g) **spinach** or **swiss chard**
milk
5 Tbsp (75 mL) **olive oil**
1 1/2 cups (375 mL) minced **onion**
4 cloves **garlic**, minced
1 cup (250 mL) **white rice**
3 Tbsp (50 mL) **white flour**
1 1/4 cups (300 mL) **parmesan cheese**
salt and **pepper** to taste
1/2 cup (125 mL) **breadcrumbs**

* Grate zucchini. Salt and set aside.
* Blanch and finely chop spinach or chard.
* Squeeze zucchini dry, reserving juice. Add milk to the juice to make 4 cups (1 L).
* Saute onion and garlic in Tbsp (25 mL) olive oil, for 5 minutes. Cover, and allow to 'sweat' 5 more minutes.
* Meanwhile, parboil rice in rapidly boiling water for 5 minutes.
* Blend flour into onion mixture and simmer 3 minutes. Add juice and bring to simmer, stirring well.
* Remove from heat. Add rice, zucchini, spinach or chard, 1 cup (250 mL) parmesan cheese, salt and pepper.
* Pour into buttered 3 qt (3 L) baking dish. Sprinkle with breadcrumbs, 1/4 cup (50 mL) parmesan cheese, and 3 Tbsp (50 mL) olive oil. Bake at 400°F (200°C) for 45–60 minutes until liquid is absorbed and top is golden-brown.

8 servings

Fisherman's Soup

1 1/4 lb (567 g) white-fleshed **fish** (cod, haddock, halibut)
3/4 lb (340 g) **shellfish** (lobster, crab, scallops, shrimp)
shells and **fish trimmings,** if available
1 cup (250 mL) **dry white wine** or **vermouth**
water
2 – 28 oz (796 mL) **canned tomatoes**
2 Tbsp (25 mL) or more **olive oil**
1 1/4 cups (300 mL) chopped **onions** (leeks and scallions, if available)
2 cloves **garlic,** mashed
1 **green pepper,** chopped
1/2 – 3/4 (125 – 175 mL) grated **carrot**
3/4 cup (175 mL) chopped **celery** (including leaves)
1/4 cup (50 mL) fresh snipped **parsley**
1/2 tsp (2 mL) **thyme**
1/2 tsp (2 mL) **basil**
1/2 tsp (2 mL) **dried fennel**
1 **bay leaf**
1 tsp (5 mL) grated **orange** or **lemon peel**
salt
pepper or **tabasco**
pinch of **saffron** (optional)
tomato paste (optional)

* Place fish, shellfish, shells and trimmings, and wine in a large soup pot. Add water to cover and simmer until fish is barely cooked, but separates from bones.
* Strain broth. Separate fish from bones and cut into small pieces. Set aside.
* Return broth to pot and add tomatoes which have been sieved. Simmer.
* Warm olive oil in a large skillet and saute onions, garlic, green pepper, carrot, and celery until softened. Cover and let *'sweat'* 5 minutes. Add to broth.
* Add: 2 Tbsp (25 mL) of parsley, and the thyme, basil, fennel, bay leaf, peel, salt and pepper or tabasco, saffron (if desired). Simmer for 15 minutes.
* Return fish to soup towards end of cooking time. Add tomato paste in small amounts to improve colour, if desired. Remove bay leaf and garnish with remaining parsley. This soup improves if allowed to stand for a while, but do not overcook fish when reheating.

8–10 servings

The Palliser
Truro

What owner Allan Bruce says about the knotty pine walls at the Palliser Restaurant aptly describes the place itself. He says the thirty-year-old pine *'just keeps getting better'*.

In 1969, Allan and Keltie Bruce bought the Palliser, a successful, conservatively run business. The pretty stucco building was a classic tourist stop, with a view of the *tidal bore*. Twice a day, a small tidal wave rushes up the Salmon River from the Bay of Fundy, past the awning-shaded picture windows of the dining room. While watching the natural attraction, tourists also patronized the restaurant and bought woolens, amethyst jewellry, and Limoges miniatures.

What the Bruces also invested in was a restaurant that ran itself in the efficient style of the former proprietor, R.L. McCurdy. A perfectionist, he set high standards for his staff in their starched white uniforms. He provided his diners a quality product in a simple and consistent way. The kitchen he designed into efficient work spaces, has not been altered at all since then.

For thirty years people have been able to count on topping off their roast lamb or chicken with a strawberry trifle dessert (Mrs. McCurdy's recipe). Over the years, the Palliser has become a place to come home to. Native son Bob Stanfield has been a regular patron over the years, as well as Ike Smith, and R.B. Cameron. Even the late John Diefenbaker had the pleasure of eating at the Palliser on two occasions.

Then there are the 'regulars'. One couple in their nineties drives up from Dartmouth every Sunday. They sit at the same table every week and request their favourite waitress. Another gentleman dines on roast lamb a dozen times a season. He claims his wife won't make it for him. In the afternoon there is a group of women who cherish a few moments away from their schedules, relaxing over a coffee and a parfait glass of maple Christmas.

What the Bruces inherited was the 'tried and true'. They have been clever to retain much of the old. But they have also made some marvellous changes.

Their 1981 renovations added considerable warmth to the dining room. They carpeted the floor, panelled the ceiling in wood, and upholstered the chairs and booths. They softly framed the windows in country flowered curtains. They divided off a room with small-paned windows, a fireplace and amber lighting, and called it the 'family room'.

The walls of this room are covered with beautifully framed photographs of Allan's and Keltie's families. Included is a relative dressed up as Napoleon for a costume ball and Keltie's MLA great-grandfather, Thomas Go-To-Bed McMullen.

In dredging up family history, after they purchased the Palliser, the Bruces discovered to their surprise and pleasure that the original Palliser Restaurant in Truro had been started by Keltie's great uncle, John McMullen. He had travelled west to Calgary. He was so impressed with the Palliser Hotel that when he returned to Truro, he named his restaurant after it. Ten years later he sold it to Mr. McCurdy, who moved it to its present site on the tidal bore.

The Bruces have also kept the 'tried and true' on the menu. Roast lamb is still a favourite and they go through 450 to 500 legs a year. Roast chicken is served with savory dressing and cranberry sauce, as always. People can rely on the lobster and club sandwiches.

But what is unusual about the menu is that not only does it have hamburger and fries made with fresh potatoes, it also lists gazpacho, escargot and chicken liver paté.

The Bruces have picked up menu ideas in their travels. While visiting Keltie's cousin, David Peel, a diplomat in Czechoslovakia, they tasted fried cheese. Jana's cheese (named after the cook who served it to them) is now on the Palliser menu (using Jarlsberg cheese). The escargot are prepared like the ones Allan tasted in Switzerland, under a pastry. They also consulted friends who were good cooks for recipe ideas. Pepper steak, flambéed in brandy, and beef burgundy have been added to the traditional fare on the menu.

It is hard to remove anything from the menu. Chocolate angel, a favourite of many people including Mr. and Mrs. Cyrus Eaton, was recently cut. Consisting of cake and ice cream smothered in chocolate sauce, it is missed. To express his dismay, one frequent diner recently brought in his own cake, and begged that it be turned into chocolate angel. Maybe, by popular demand, the Palliser will be forced to put it back on the menu. It's hard to break a tradition like that.

Strawberry Trifle

This is an original McCurdy recipe. Although the Palliser serves it in individual parfait glasses, you may wish to bring it uncut to the table, in a large serving dish, as a dramatic splash at the end of a dinner party.

Bake the sponge cake first. While it is in the oven, cook the custard. When both are cool, whip the cream and assemble the trifle.

Sponge Cake

1 1/2 cups (375 mL) **white flour**
1 Tbsp (15 mL) **baking powder**
1/2 tsp (2 mL) **salt**
12 Tbsp (175 mL) **white sugar**
6 **eggs,** separated
1/4 cup (50 mL) **cold water**
1 tsp (5 mL) **lemon rind**
2 tsp (10 mL) fresh **lemon juice**
1 tsp (5 mL) **vanilla**

* Line the bottom of a 8" x 8" (19.7 cm x 19.7 cm) cake pan with wax paper. Butter paper.
* Sift together: flour, baking powder, salt, and 6 Tbsp (100 mL) sugar.
* Beat egg whites until stiff. Beat in 2 Tbsp (25 mL) sugar.
* In a separate bowl, beat the egg yolks, water, lemon rind, and lemon juice until thick and fluffy (5 minutes with an electric mixer). Add 4 Tbsp (50 mL) sugar and vanilla and beat a minute more.
* Add flour mixture to make a smooth batter. As it will be thick and sticky, finish this by hand.
* Stir in 1 cup (250 mL) of egg whites to lighten mixture. Gently fold in remaining egg whites.
* Pour in prepared pan and bake at 300°F (150°C) for 45 minutes.

Custard

1/2 cup (125 mL) **white sugar**
3 Tbsp (50 mL) **cornstarch**
4 **egg yolks**
3 cups (750 mL) **milk**
1 tsp (5 mL) **vanilla**

* Combine sugar and cornstarch in a heavy-bottomed saucepan. Whisk in egg yolks until blended. Add milk and cook over medium-low heat, stirring constantly until thickened. Remove from heat and add vanilla.

To assemble the trifle:

Sponge cake
Custard
1/4 cup (50 mL) **sherry**
1/2 cup (125 mL) **strawberry jam**
2 cups (500 mL) **whipping cream**
1 cup (250 mL) fresh or frozen **strawberries**

* Remove paper from cooled cake. Slice cake horizontally into two layers.
* Whip 1 cup (250 mL) whipping cream.
* Place bottom layer of cake in a deep, nonmetallic serving dish or bowl (sides at least 5" (13 cm) high).
* Sprinkle with sherry and spread on jam and whipped cream.
* Place top layer on cake. Spoon custard over cake. Cover with plastic wrap and chill at least 4 hours or overnight.
* Before serving: Whip remaining cup (250 mL) cream. Slice or defrost strawberries.
* To serve, top with a dollop of whipped cream and strawberry garnish.

8–10 servings

Roadside Grill
Belliveau Cove

Travelling from Yarmouth to Digby along the ribbon of road commonly known as *the French shore*, one is struck by the quiet beauty of domestic order. The end of one small village flows into the beginning of the next, with no break in the countryside, except for the open blue expanse of St. Mary's Bay. There is a poetic rhythm to the names which repeat themselves on the mailboxes along the road — Amirault, Belliveau, Boudreau, Comeau, Deveau, Robicheau, Thibodeau. Therefore, it comes as a surprise, when stopping for a bite at the Roadside Grill in Belliveau Cove, to read the proprietors' names on the side of the building — *the Hawerychuks.*

Cora Bonnenfant grew up in Belliveau Cove with her ten brothers and sisters. At twenty-four, she decided she needed a change. She went on a holiday to visit one of her brothers who had moved to Oshawa, Ontario. Meanwhile, James Hawerychuk had also found his way there from Wynford, Saskatchewan, and his family of fifteen brothers and sisters. He found work in the General Motors plant. They met on a blind date, fell in love and stayed in Oshawa until 1968. That year they bought D'Eon's Restaurant and Cabins, and with their two children moved back to Cora's home of Belliveau Cove. Soon after, James learned how to make rappie pie.

The Roadside Grill is an old fashioned, cozy kind of place. Except for a coat of white enamel on the board and batten walls, the decor has not changed much since it was built in 1926. There are three scrupulously clean rooms with a kitchen behind.

In the main room is an old wooden store counter with a curved glass display case. The walls are covered with stuffed heads of animals who have not cavorted in the woods in decades. The pencilled date on the back of the bobcat indicates it was shot in 1939, the lynx in 1928, the deer in 1939.

In the two small adjoining rooms are homemade (but very comfortable) wooden booths painted white and chocolate brown. When it is not foggy, large windows let in extravagant amounts of sunshine. It is a cheerful spot.

Also displayed proudly are James's certificates, his membership in "Chevalier de Colomb" and the Kinsmen. As well, there are two photographs of James and a handsome young hockey player, his nephew Dale Hawerchuk who plays for the Winnipeg Jets.

The Roadside Grill is a good place to stop for lunch. If the menu is simple and unpretentious, then so are the prices. A bowl of homemade fish chowder is priced at $1.50, a piece of pie, $1.00.

Sandwiches do well, as does the seafood. The fish is freshly caught and brought in a few miles down the road. They go through gallons of raw shucked clams, for the fried clams and rappie pie. These are also supplied locally.

James has become somewhat an expert at making traditional Acadian potato pie. He makes up quantities of rappie pie using pails and pails of potatoes every day. He has come up with an alternative to the tedious grating and hand squeezing of the pulp, which is involved in the conventional method. He uses an electric juicer, which grates and separates the juices simultaneously. To fill his rappie pies, James uses either raw clams, chicken, beef or when available, wild meat like deer or rabbit.

The Roadside Grill is open all year round, but the Hawerychuks, who live upstairs, usually close down after lunch, until the supper hour. They have a nice steady little business. It is interesting that James, from Saskatchewan, makes some of his living preparing Acadian food. But there are two sides to the coin. Over the years, Cora has learned how to make cabbage rolls, and perfect Ukranian perogies.

Fish Chowder

Cora says that the chowder will keep well in the fridge for three days if the milk is not added until it is ready to be eaten.

1/2 cup (125 mL) **butter**
1/4 cup (50 mL) diced **onion**
1/2 cup (125 mL) **water**
6 **potatoes**
water to cover
1 lb (454 g) **fish:** haddock, clams, scallops or combination
1 cup (250 mL) **milk**
salt and **pepper** to taste

* Melt butter in a dutch oven and saute onions for a few minutes.
* Add 1/2 cup (125 mL) water and simmer a few minutes.
* Peel and dice potatoes. Add to dutch oven with water to cover. Bring to a boil. Reduce heat, cover and simmer 15–20 minutes until tender but not mushy.
* Cut the fish into bite-size portions and add to soup. Cook over medium heat until fish is opaque. Add milk, salt and pepper. Heat but do not allow to boil.

6 servings

Rappie Pie

In this traditional Acadian potato pie, the potatoes are grated and the liquid and potato starch are separated from the pulp. The liquid is replaced with chicken, meat or clam broth. The texture of the potatoes changes significantly. Although Mr. Hawerychuk uses an electric juicer to separate pulp from liquid, in this recipe, the quantities are small enough that hand squeezing will not be a burden.

2 lb (1 kg) **chicken parts**
2 medium **onions**
water
1/2 tsp (2 mL) **salt**
1/2 tsp (2 mL) **pepper**
2 Tbsp (25 mL) **lard**
14 medium **potatoes**
2 Tbsp (25 mL) **butter**
2 Tbsp (25 mL) **white flour**

* Place chicken in a medium saucepan with 1 onion, salt, pepper and water to cover. Bring to a boil. Reduce heat, cover and simmer for one hour.
* Cool. Remove chicken and separate meat from bones.
* Finely dice remaining onion and fry in lard until translucent. Set aside.
* Peel and finely grate potatoes. Stir to release as much liquid as possible.
* Take handfuls of grated potato and squeeze. Reserve and measure liquid.
* Place dry grated pulp in a large dutch oven. Add fried onions and lard. Stir in 1/2 cup (125 mL) *cold* water to break up lumps.
* Measure an amount of chicken broth equal to potato liquid (approximately 1 2/3 cups (400 mL). Reheat.
* Pour hot broth over grated potato, stirring constantly. Keep stirring over medium heat until potatoes become translucent (almost jelly-like) and come away from the sides of the pot in one mass. Add salt and pepper to taste.
* Butter and flour a baking pan 8" x 8" (19.7 cm x 19.7 cm). Pour a 1" (2.5 cm) layer of potato in the pan. Add a layer of deboned chicken. Top with remaining potato. Dot with butter.
* Bake at 425°F (220°C) for 1-1 1/2 hours until crusty brown.

8 servings

Telegraph House
Baddeck

When Mary Dunlop married her husband, she became the fourth Mrs. Dunlop to host the Telegraph House in Baddeck. *'We are the fourth generation to manage the inn, and our children will be the fifth,'* she says with quiet confidence.

There was a Mrs. Dunlop who welcomed Charles Dudley Warner to Baddeck around 1870. He described the Telegraph House in his book *Baddeck and that Sort of Thing*, published in 1896, as *'a very unhotel-like appearing hotel'*, with flower garden in front, *'blazing with welcome lights'*.

A Mrs. Dunlop also offered hospitality to Alexander Graham Bell and family in 1885 and years after. So entranced with the area, they finally built their famous summer home Beinn Bhreagh.

Hospitality comes naturally to Mary Dunlop. Her policy is to keep a lump of Inverness coal burning all the time in the fireplace of the main livingroom. *'The girls have to learn how to make a fire just as well as they wait on tables'*, she notes. The fireplace is surrounded by photographs of her family. On the mantel are her prized family girondoles, table chandeliers with drop-shaped prisms.

Food at the Telegraph House also seems to be a matter of tradition. Where else but in Cape Breton could one order a basket of oatcakes and a cup of tea for $1.50. Mrs. Dunlop says, *'we take our tea seriously'*. By this she means that the water must be heated in a proper kettle and steeped the right length of time.

While the oatcake recipe is *'as old as the house'*, many of the dishes served in the restaurant are from old recipes, too. Mrs. Dunlop inherited her mother-in-law's tattered cook books.

Salmon is poached and served in an old fashioned egg sauce. Cold salmon sandwiches (not of the ordinary canned variety) are made from this same poached salmon and served on chewy, yeasty homemade bread.

The Telegraph House has its own variety of fish chowder. It is made with halibut, scallops, clams and haddock, but also has little flecks of green pepper and orange. The salmon tidbits make it very pretty.

The kitchen is a large, commercial space, but much home style cooking goes on there. Mrs. Dunlop is proud they use no canned bases. All their stocks are made from fresh beef and ham. In the fall, they make up large batches of pickled cucumbers, beets, chows and applesauce for use in the restaurant. In another season rhubarb is picked fresh and frozen. It later finds its way into the rhubarb dessert cake.

In February 1984, Prince Michael, brother of the Duke of Kent, came to Baddeck to celebrate the 75th anniversary of the flight of the Silver Dart. It was the first heavier-than-air machine to be flown in the British Empire.

With a history of hospitality toward the Bell family, the Telegraph House was chosen to host a reception sponsored by the Silver Dart Committee in honour of His Royal Highness. Mrs. Dunlop served a meal worthy of royalty. She chose a menu of consomme, steamed scallops with French wine and cheese, and lemon chiffon delight.

Protocol officers from both federal and provincial governments arrived to help her with the arrangements. They didn't always agree! But they had a test run to iron out any problems, complete with food, people, table setting, serving and dining. Everything and everyone was there except the prince. Things went off without a hitch. Mrs. Dunlop relaxed, in the knowledge that when the prince and his entourage of fifteen arrived, things would go smoothly. But when she glanced at the main table, she noticed that it lacked something special to make it fit for a prince. Acting on a final bit inspiration, she went into the living room and took down her beautiful girondoles from the fireplace mantel. Mrs. Dunlop set them on the table and they looked lovely.

Poached Salmon with Egg Sauce

4–8 1" (2.5 cm) thick **salmon steaks** (enough for 4 people)
2 **eggs**
1 1/2 Tbsp (22 mL) **butter**
2 cups (500 mL) **milk**
1 1/2 Tbsp (22 mL) **white flour**
1 1/2 Tbsp (22 mL) **cornstarch**
salt and **pepper**
lemon wedges (optional)

* Hard boil eggs. Peel, slice and set aside.
* Heat butter and 1 3/4 cups (425 mL) milk in a double boiler.
* Combine flour and cornstarch. Stir in 1/4 cup (75 mL) milk to make a smooth paste.
* Whisk paste into the hot milk, stirring constantly until thickened. Season with salt and pepper to taste and stir in eggs. Keep warm while poaching salmon.
* Bring a large pan of salted water to a boil. Gently immerse the steaks in the water. Immediately reduce the heat to simmer. Steaks should be cooked in 5–8 minutes. Do not overcook.
* Remove from water. Spoon on egg sauce and garnish with lemon wedges.

4 servings

Poor Man's Pudding

In this sweet old fashioned dessert, the spongy cake rises to the top while the brown sugar sauce bubbles up from the bottom.

1/3 cup (75 mL) **shortening**
1 cup (250 mL) **white sugar**
2 cups (500 mL) **flour**
1 tsp (5 mL) **baking powder**
1/4 tsp (1 mL) **salt**
1/2 cup (125 mL) **milk**
1 1/3 cups (325 mL) **brown sugar**
1 cup (250 mL) **coconut**
3 cups (750 mL) **hot water**

* Cream shortening and white sugar.
* Sift together: flour, baking powder, and salt. Add flour mixture to shortening, alternately with milk. Blend to make a soft dough.
* Pat the dough into a buttered 8" x 8" (19.7 cm x 19.7 cm) cake pan, or casserole. Sprinkle on brown sugar and coconut. Pour on hot water.
* Bake at 350°F (180°C) for 50 minutes until golden brown.

8 good sized servings

Scottish Oat Cakes

Neither cookie nor biscuit, these traditional Cape Breton goodies are wonderful with a dab of jam and a cup o' tea. Watch them carefully, as they burn easily.

1/2 tsp (2 mL) **baking soda**
1/2 cup (125 mL) **boiling water**
1 1/4 cups (300 mL) **white sugar**
2 cups (500 mL) **rolled oats**
2 cups (500 mL) **white flour**
1 tsp (5 mL) **baking powder**
1 tsp (5 mL) **salt**
2 cups (500 mL) **bran**
1 1/4 cups (300 mL) **shortening**

* Dissolve soda in boiling water and set aside.
* Mix together: sugar, oats, flour, baking powder, salt, bran.
* Cut in shortening and stir in water. Form into a ball.
* Roll out on a floured surface to a thickness of 1/8"–1/4". Cut into 2" (1 cm) squares.
* Place on lightly greased cookie sheets. Bake at 425°F (220°C) for 10–12 minutes until brown.

Yield: 40 – 2"x2" (5 cm x 5 cm) squares or more if rolled thinner

The Whitman Inn
Kempt

The Whitman Inn is for people who wish they had cousins to visit in the country. The atmosphere is relaxed and comfortable in the big old rambling house, crammed with period pieces of lumbering mission oak, auction memorabilia and Morris chairs. The kitchen is cozy, complete with a Peacock wood cook stove and rocking chair. The dining area is a pretty room with red ochre wainscotting, hand-painted stencilled walls and a screen door onto the porch.

Three years ago, Nancy and Bruce Gurnham came upon a beat up old house that had been abandoned for over a decade, and took pity on it. They had visions of the empty rooms filled with life and activity. So they proceeded to turn their lives around to bring about this happy transformation. Leaving high stress jobs in the United States behind them, and with the help of family, they scrambled to get the place functioning by the summer of 1982. Today the inn is filled with the hustle and bustle of not only guests, but also of the three young children the Gurnhams recently adopted.

Nancy says, '*We wanted a place where people with a family could come and enjoy themselves, and that they could afford*'. Her family style hospitality shows in the parlor where there is not only an eclectic collection of books for adult enjoyment, but also a toy corner for children.

Dinners at the Whitman Inn are not fancy, but helpings are large and wholesome. Generally the main entree of chicken, fish or meat is chosen by the first person to telephone and make a reservation. Nancy fills in the rest of the menu. She usually includes a soup, homemade bread, salad and dessert. A nurse by profession, Nancy is happy to accommodate people on diets such as diabetics, coronary patients and vegetarians.

Although a local woman sometimes serves the dinner, all the food preparation and clean-up is done by the Gurnham family. The children are proud to help out. Nancy does her cooking on a standard 30" electric range in the summer. In the winter she enjoys cooking on her wood stove. She says she serves her guests what she likes to cook, which is good nutritious food made '*from scratch*'. She is a self taught cook who has learned a lot from her large cook book collection ranging from Julia Child to *Moosewood*.

Fairly isolated from suppliers, the Gurnhams travel far for their groceries. They drive to the South Shore for fresh fish, and belong to a food co-op for dry ingredients, such as the stone ground flour essential to Nancy's whole wheat bread. They are lucky to have a

good local butcher, but travel the 100 or so miles to Halifax for get their just-right blend of coffee beans.

But the travel is worth it because coffee and tea are an important part of Whitman Inn hospitality. Guests are offered fourteen varieties of herbal and imported teas or coffee from beans that have been ground specially with a bit of cinnamon bark. Sitting back after a nice meal, diners are pressed to have a second or even third cup of brew. They are hard to turn down, not just because the beverages are good, but because Nancy's warm freckled smiles accompany them.

Marinated Loin of Pork

This is not a marinade in the usual sense since it contains no liquid. The dry salting infuses flavour into the meat. Use the lesser or greater amount of salt according to your taste preference.

1-5 tsp (5-25 mL) **salt**
1 1/8 tsp (7 mL) freshly ground **pepper**
1 1/4 tsp (7 mL) **thyme**
1 1/4 tsp (7 mL) **sage**
1/2 tsp (2 mL) ground **allspice**
2 **bay leaves,** crumbled
3 **garlic cloves,** finely minced
1/2 cup (125 mL) chopped **green onions**
3-5 lb (1 1/2 - 2 1/2 kg) boned **pork loin roast**
Butcher's twine for retying roast

* Blend all ingredients except roast, in a large glass or nonreactive bowl.
* Untie roast. Place in bowl, rubbing mixture into meat. Cover and refrigerate 24 hours. Turn several times to redistribute juices, during this time.
* Discard juices drawn out by salt. Dry meat thoroughly. Retie with butcher's twine.
* Sear on all sides. Bake in a covered roaster at 325°F (160°C) for 2-3 hours until internal temperature reaches 160°F (71°C).

4-6 servings

Dutch Babies

Nancy says children especially love these "babies", or oven baked pancakes. Serve them with maple syrup, jam, fruit, sour cream, peanut butter, or whatever you have on hand.

2 Tbsp (25 mL) **butter**
4 **eggs**
1 cup (250 mL) **milk**
1/2 tsp (2 mL) **vanilla**
1/2 cup (125 mL) **white flour**
3 Tbsp (50 mL) **white sugar**
1/2 tsp (2 mL) **salt**

* Melt butter and grease two – 10" (25 cm) glass pie plates.
* Whisk together: eggs, milk, and vanilla. Add flour, sugar and salt and blend well.
* Pour into pie plates. Bake at 400°F (200°C) for 20 minutes until puffed and golden. They will deflate when the steam escapes, so serve immediately.

2–3 servings

Zwicker's Inn
Mahone Bay

Jack Sorenson, of Zwicker's Inn calls a noodle a noodle, not pasta or fettucine. There is no vichyssoise on the menu either. Sorenson calls leek and potato soup just that. He says a conscious effort has been made to *'remove all intimidating details'* and pretension from his restaurant.

What is more important to Sorenson is the process by which the flour, moistened with egg and water is transformed into noodles and served to restaurant guests. The dough is kneaded, rolled and cut in the Zwicker kitchen. The raw noodles are stirred into the vigorously boiling water just a few minutes before serving, to be in optimum condition, neither gummy nor overcooked. They are gloriously garnished with a combination of shrimp, lemon, cream and dill or perhaps mushrooms, butter and parmesan. The noodles are treated with respect, not as a bland medium for an overwhelming sauce.

The lowly noodle may be treated with more regard than is usual, but so is every foodstuff that is prepared in this kitchen. From the perfect butter rosebuds, to the steaming freshness of the coffee, the owners *'care intensely'* (as stated on the back of the menu) that the *'food and service be excellent and of full value'*.

Jack and Katherine Sorenson set aside careers as professional musicians to manage Zwicker's Inn. Their piano, which takes up a good portion of their office, is often covered with business papers, but their unique establishment is a reflection of its meticulous musician owners. Sorenson, who was also a music producer at CBC has brought a special sense of programming to their venture.

The Zwicker dining room includes three small, simply furnished rooms. Watercolours, African violets, and flowered curtains all contribute to a feeling of casual elegance. The staff is articulate. Diners feel taken care of, but not interfered with in this serene white and yellow space.

Up on the second floor, it is a different matter. Renovating within the constraints of an early nineteenth century building, the Sorensons have designed an efficient if crowded kitchen capable of producing, from scratch, 250 meals a day.

They have been inventive in many ways. A box with a hot plate built in, keeps serving dishes piping hot. Collapsible counters fit in and slip out, making them dual purpose. A small portable sink fits into a hole in the counter when noodles need to be drained. A washer-spin dryer centrifically forces the water out of a vat of greens. The ice cream maker, which turns out small batches of superb lime-honey ice cream in just twenty minutes, is a home concocted chest freezer juiced up with antifreeze.

The kitchen is filled with staff, who if not professionally trained, follow Sorenson's instructions to the letter. And his instructions are very specific indeed.

In the off season, Sorenson *practises* his cooking. He is a gifted chef, who works at his recipes and techniques. His mussel soup, which the menu unabashedly says is based on a soup from Maxim's of Paris, is a good example. *'I start with the basic recipe and note a "hole" in the flavour'*, he says. He experiments with it until he finds the ingredient to fill the gap. He continues to work at it, honing it down to make the most efficient use of ingredients and the cook's time. He even simplifies it to reduce the number of dirty pots and pans incurred. Once the formula is perfected, it is passed on to the staff, for performance.

Great use is made of posted instructions, premeasured amounts, timers and a constant 400°F oven. Using prime ingredients, following Sorenson's techniques and procedures, and repeating patterns over and over again, results in the Zwicker's chief component of success — consistently prepared high quality cuisine.

The food is superb. The menu offers a wide variety of choices. A meal can be made of appetizers alone, including five soups such as tomato bisque and seafood chowder. The ten appetizers include Sorenson's own version of Solomon Gundy, and an unusual mushroom-almond paté. Whole lemon-steamed mussels are accompanied by a much needed finger bowl.

The fifteen or so main dishes are listed on the menu with ample descriptions. It's hard to order any one of them without knowing what you are getting into. The beef tenderloin is cooked in a sauce described as *'tangy but not astonishing'*. The *'heavenly chicken'* comes with a preamble listing all of its ingredients; sour cream, white wine, mushrooms, shallots.

The desserts are also Sorenson originals. The ice creams are world class and are served with a delicate butter cookie. The Nova Scotia Rum Sundae is a gorgeous conglomerate of textures and flavours; cold ice cream, warm rum, crunchy toasted nuts and smooth whipping cream. No matter how full people may feel after dinner, they usually manage to squeeze in one of the delectable desserts.

This restaurant is not just a happy accident, but a conscious effort by the owners to provide the public with health giving, decent nourishment. Strict vegetarians until one week before opening the restaurant in 1980, the Sorensons feel a responsibility towards the people they feed. Sorenson says he considers his guests *'special'* and *'appreciative'* of what he does.

What he and Katherine have done, is orchestrate a system for producing large volumes of food in an institutional setting, without compromising results. They don't add artificial or masking flavours because the ingredients they use have not been diminished by freezing, canning, steaming and other quantity processing techniques.

One successful staple of Zwicker's is bread. Sorenson says there is nothing magic about their much requested recipe. The outstanding flavour comes from the whole grain flour which is ground, in the kitchen, the morning the bread is baked. Simple — there are no substitutions, no shortcuts.

Much of the success of Zwicker's Inn comes down to the use of fresh, natural ingredients which are combined with a measure of respect. Strange, in this day of microwaves, margarine and blast frozen berries, that more restaurants don't know this secret.

Mussel Soup

4 lb (1800 g) fresh live **mussels** in shell
1/2 cup (125 mL) **water**
1/4 cup (50 mL) **butter**
1 1/2 cups (375 mL) **white wine**
5 grinds fresh **pepper**
1 1/2 oz (40 g) medium-fine minced **shallots**
1 cup (250 mL) minced **onion**
5 **egg yolks**
2 cups (500 mL) **whipping cream**
2 Tbsp (25 mL) **dried parsley**

* Scrub mussels under running water and scrape off beards. Put mussels and water in a large saucepan over medium-high heat. Cover and shake pan frequently until mussels open.
* Strain broth into a measuring cup and add water, if necessary, to measure 4 cups (1 L). Separate meat from shells.
* Stew together: butter, wine, pepper, shallots, and onion over medium heat for 10 minutes. Add broth.
* Beat egg yolks until creamy and blend with whipping cream.
* Heat mussel broth in a large saucepan. Add hot broth to egg mixture, 1/4 cup (50 mL) at a time. Stir constantly until half the broth has been added. Pour back into large saucepan, combining broth and eggs into one pan.
* Add mussels. Bring to near boil. Reduce to simmer and stir constantly for 5 minutes. Add parsley.

8 servings

Lime-Honey Ice Cream

Super smooth home-made ice cream has made Zwicker's Inn famous. As an interesting difference, Jack Sorenson substitutes honey for the usual sugar. Feel free to double the recipe.

3 Tbsp (50 mL) **white flour**
1 1/2 cups (375 mL) **milk**
1 cup (250 mL) **honey**
2 cups (500 mL) **whipping cream**
1/2 cup (125 mL) **fresh lime juice**
2 tsp (10 mL) grated **lime rind**

* Place flour in a heavy bottomed saucepan. Gradually whisk in milk to a smooth consistency.
* Place over medium-low heat. Stir constantly until thickened. Strain to remove any lumps.
* While still warm, whisk in honey until melted and well blended. Stir in whipping cream and lime juice. Chill.
* Churn-freeze according to manufacturers' instructions. After freezing, stir in lime rind.

Yield: 6 cups (1 1/2 L)